Leading
High-Performance
School Systems

MARC TUCKER

Leading
High-Performance
School Systems

Lessons from the World's Best

Alexandria, Virginia USA

NCEE
National Center On
EDUCATION
And The Economy

Washington, DC USA

1703 N. Beauregard St.
Alexandria, VA 22311-1714 USA
Phone: 800-933-2723 or 703-578-9600
Fax: 703-575-5400
Website: www.ascd.org
E-mail: member@ascd.org
Author guidelines: www.ascd.org/write

2121 K Street NW, Suite 700
Washington, DC 20037
Phone: 202-379-1800
Fax: 202-293-1560
Website: www.NCEE.org

Deborah S. Delisle, *Executive Director*; Stefani Roth, *Publisher*; Genny Ostertag, *Director, Content Acquisitions*; Susan Hills, *Acquisitions Editor*; Julie Houtz, *Director, Book Editing & Production*; Joy Scott Ressler, *Editor*; Judi Connelly, *Associate Art Director*; Georgia Park, *Senior Graphic Designer*; Cynthia Stock, *Typesetter*; Mike Kalyan, *Director, Production Services*; Shajuan Martin, *E-Publishing Specialist*; Kelly Marshall, *Senior Production Specialist*

Published simultaneously by ASCD and the National Center on Education and the Economy.

PAPERBACK ISBN: 978-1-4166-2700-5   ASCD product #118055   n1/19
PDF E-BOOK ISBN: 978-1-4166-2702-9; see Books in Print for other formats.

Quantity discounts are available: e-mail programteam@ascd.org or call 800-933-2723, ext. 5773, or 703-575-5773. For desk copies, go to www.ascd.org/deskcopy.

Library of Congress Cataloging-in-Publication Data

Names: Tucker, Marc S., author.
Title: Leading high-performance school systems : lessons from the world's best / Marc Tucker.
Description: Alexandria, VA : ASCD, [2019] | Includes bibliographical references and index. |
Identifiers: LCCN 2018030055 (print) | LCCN 2018046503 (ebook) | ISBN 9781416627029 (PDF) | ISBN 9781416627005 (pbk.)
Subjects: LCSH: Educational leadership—United States. | Educational change—United States.
Classification: LCC LB2805 (ebook) | LCC LB2805 .T84 2019 (print) | DDC 371.2—dc23
LC record available at https://lccn.loc.gov/2018030055

27 26 25 24 23 22 21 20 19   1 2 3 4 5 6 7 8 9 10 11 12

Leading High-Performance School Systems

Lessons from the World's Best

Foreword

Americans are known around the world as innovators—something that is as true in education as it is in medicine, business, and technology. Visit any of the top-ranked places of the world—Singapore, Shanghai, Canada, or Finland—and examine pioneering practices in teaching, educator preparation, or assessment, and you will no doubt be told about US origins for many of their reforms.

However, rather than allowing these practices to remain as boutique exceptions to the rule, these countries have taken good ideas from the US, from other countries, and from their own experiences and have used them to transform their systems of education. They not only scale up good ideas, they also build on what they have learned from processes of continuous improvement over time, rather than shifting ideologies and policies with the pendulum swings of politics.

In short, they build *systems* of education that create a foundation of adequate, well-directed resources; strong teaching; and thoughtful curriculum and assessment for *all* schools, not just for a lucky few. In this important book, Marc Tucker describes how this system-building is accomplished. Tucker has been studying and describing systems for many years, helping to shape the understanding of both policymakers and practitioners who are on a quest to ensure that all children learn to high levels and have the opportunity to fulfill their potential.

At the start of this book, he notes how hard U.S. educators are working to try to make progress. "That's because the system—designed a century ago to solve a very different set of problems than the ones the nation now faces—does not work anymore. Simply managing current systems is getting harder and harder. That will continue until we replace them with systems that are much better adapted to the challenges we now face."

These challenges include the need for a much more highly educated populace—making available to virtually all students the kind of thinking curriculum once available to a very small elite—and the need for teaching that can address the wide diversity of student experiences and needs in US schools. This requires a much more systematic and serious set of investments in the training of teachers and school leaders, so that all of them can be as well-prepared as the best currently are. It also requires an infrastructure of ongoing learning supports, including cultivation and recognition of teaching expertise in ways that allow it to be tapped in all schools.

Over the course of his career, Marc Tucker has made extraordinary contributions to developing these kinds of learning supports in the US: During the 1980s, he was responsible, with the Carnegie Corporation of New York, for the launch of the National Board for Professional Teaching Standards—the first body to convene accomplished teachers to develop standards for the profession and to create authentic assessments of teaching to certify accomplished teaching. In the last two decades, numerous studies have confirmed that Board-certified teachers are generally more effective than others, and that these teachers contribute to greater effectiveness for other teachers in their buildings. Board-certified teachers often observe that engaging in the process of certification was one of the most powerful learning experiences of their career—and one that changed their approach to teaching forever.

The Board's standards became the stimulus for similar initiatives all over the globe, and standards articulating what teachers should know and be able to do are now found in every leading nation as a framework for systematically guiding teacher recruitment, preparation, induction, ongoing professional learning, appraisal and feedback. In places like Singapore and Shanghai, they also guide the design of career ladders that develop expert teachers for all schools, so that the best teachers can serve as mentors and coaches for other teachers.

A few states in the US have, at moments in time, taken this kind of systematic approach to teaching standards, built an infrastructure for training that incorporates the standards, and even built in incentives for teachers to become Board-certified. As I described in *The Flat World and Education*, states like Connecticut and North Carolina that invested in standards-based reforms of teaching realized large gains in student achievement as a result of their efforts in the 1990s.

However, most states have continued to operate fragmented non-systems which allow substantial variability in the standards teachers meet before entry and substantial quality differentials across preparation institutions, fail to connect preparation with ongoing evaluation and professional development, and lack any means for recognizing and taking advantage of Board-certified teachers' skills, leaving these talented certified teachers "all dressed up with no place to go."

Equally important are the skills of school leaders to create systems of support for high-quality teaching. Seeing little training infrastructure available in the United States to help school principals learn these skills, Tucker and his National Center on Education and the Economy created the National Institute for School Leadership (NISL), now the largest program to train school leaders in the United States. Building on the best research on student learning and teacher development to create effective schools focused on 21st century skills, NISL is designed to give school superintendents, central office staff and principals the skills they need to design and run the kind of high performance schools and school systems described in this book .

A few years ago, Tucker and his team were asked by the National Conference of State Legislatures to support the work of a study group composed of state legislators assembled to report back to the whole association on the strategies used by the countries with the most successful education systems The result was a volume titled *No Time to Lose*, the biggest selling report in the history of the NCSL. The report succeeded in sounding the alarm by describing not only how far ahead of the states these countries are, and what is at stake, but also what states needed to do to catch up by putting all the policy components of high performing systems—early childhood education, curriculum and assessment, resource distribution, teaching and school leadership, college and career readiness—in place. Tucker and NCEE are now working with the state of Maryland to help build this kind of high performance education system. This work will hopefully help transform what is often an inchoate set of political decisions that bump around like a ball in a pinball machine into decisions that can instantiate a coherent approach to supporting schools that can, in turn, support teachers to teach and students to learn.

The roadmap for this work is here in this book. Here, Marc Tucker draws on the accumulated wisdom of his own decades of research and scholarly activism—and the research he has commissioned by others, including myself—to shed light on key aspects of a system that functions to prepare all students for the rapidly changing, knowledge-based world they are entering. The book is a magnum opus, a compilation of the best research, thinking, and action of pioneering educators around the world, including Tucker himself. Grippingly written, persuasively argued, and vivid in its examples, this account will provide readers with a clear set of ideas about what is educationally possible, why it is necessary, and what we should do about it. The result of this analyses deserves our attention because, indeed, in this era when the fate of societies, as well as individuals, depends on their capacity to learn, we have no time to lose.

Linda Darling-Hammond
Stanford, CA, November 23, 2018

Preface

There has never been a more frustrating time to be a school leader in the United States, whether you are a superintendent of schools, a central office executive, or a school principal. That's because the system—designed a century ago to solve a very different set of problems than the ones the nation now faces—does not work anymore. Simply managing current systems is getting harder and harder. That will continue until we replace them with systems that are much better adapted to the challenges we now face. But there has also never been a more exciting time to be a superintendent, a central office executive, or a principal. That's because the people who will be designing the new system that can respond to today's challenges will be you, today's school leaders.

We wrote this book to help you understand the forces that have made the current system obsolete, to give you some insight into the way the world's leading education systems are tackling today's education challenges, and to help you gain the knowledge and skills you will need to design and build education systems that will be as effective at meeting the coming challenges as *any* in the world.

The book was written by the author with a lot of help from a team from the National Center on Education and the Economy, an organization that for almost 30 years has been studying the global economy and the countries with the most successful education systems. You might reasonably ask about our name. The connection—between the economy and education—has everything to do with why we wrote this book.

For a century, the United States led the world in public education. Borrowing a page from the Prussians, the United States extended the right to a free public elementary school education to youngsters throughout the country in the mid-19th century. Half a century later, the United States did it again with secondary education. And then, after World War II, the nation opened up higher education to the masses. Everywhere else it had been reserved for the privileged few.

By the 1960s, the United States had the world's most highly educated workforce. Economists have shown that this vast, unprecedented expansion of education was a major cause, maybe even the most important cause, of this country's remarkable economic rise at the end of the 19th century (Goldin & Katz, 2008).

By the mid-20th century, the United States was essentially operating a two-tiered system: one that provided what has been called a "thinking curriculum" for an elite minority of students bound for four-year colleges, professional work, and management jobs; and a basic-skills curriculum for everyone else. For much of the 20th century, this system worked fine: most jobs were in retail, manufacturing, mining, and farming, and back in those days, what most workers needed to do those jobs was basic literacy in English and mathematics. Schools were expected to provide students with those skills, give some of them rudimentary vocational skills, and socialize immigrant children into the American melting pot. Before the GI Bill, relatively few went on to four-year colleges and those who did were quickly absorbed into the labor market. As the U.S. economy flourished, all boats rose at once. Those with college educations did very well, but the much larger number with just the basic skills did well enough, especially in manufacturing, to become solid members of the middle class, living, typically, far better than their parents had.

But then the dynamics of the global economy changed. Advances in communications and shipping technology made it possible to locate manufacturing far from the countries where the manufactured products were to be sold. By then, many developing countries were doing as good a job as the United States at educating their citizens in the basic skills, but their workers were paid as little as one one-hundredth what U.S. workers with the same skills were charging. Millions of jobs went overseas, leaving the people who had those jobs out of work or forcing them to work for a small fraction of what they had previously earned. Manufacturers that failed to relocate their manufacturing operations overseas were often forced out of business (Commission on the Skills of the American Workforce, 1990).

Those changes in the way the global economy worked—as profound and as consequential for millions of Americans as they were—paled in comparison to what was coming: enormous advances in digital technology that are now accounting for the loss of many more jobs than outsourcing ever did (Friedman, 2007). Parallel advances in cognitive psychology, artificial intelligence, neural networks, natural language processing, sensors, robotics, and allied fields, combined with logarithmic advances in processing speed, memory capacity, and networking, have produced advances that could make a quarter to a half of the current workforce very vulnerable—unemployed, unemployable, or employable only at poverty wages—before today's 1st graders have been in the workforce for 10 years (Brynholfsson & McAffee, 2014; Ford, 2015).

We are describing the young people who actually *have* the basic skills our system was designed to produce in most of our high school graduates. But large numbers of young people graduate or fail to graduate without acquiring those skills.

The challenge now is unprecedented. *American educators must figure out how to provide to all a kind and quality of education that educators have provided up to now only to a small elite.* They will have to raise average academic performance of students graduating high school two to three grade levels above the current average while substantially closing the gaps between the top performers and the bottom performers, and they will need to do all of this for not much more money than schools are now spending.

That, you will say, is impossible. But it isn't impossible. How do we know that? Because high school students in a growing number of countries—close to 30 now—are outperforming U.S. high school students, many of them by the kinds of margins we just described (OECD, 2016b).[1] In the 1970s, the century-long climb in the number of years of education for the average U.S. worker had come to an end. But the number of years for the average worker in other industrial countries had not only caught up to the United States; it continued to climb and eventually surpassed the United States. When researchers began testing students in different countries with the same tests, they discovered that high school students in those countries not only had more years of education but were *better* educated than those in the United States. In fact, the most recent research shows that millennials in the U.S. workforce, once the best educated in the world, are now among the least well educated in the industrialized world (Goodman, Sands, & Coley, 2017)

That is very bad news for the United States, because the amount and quality of the education you have—whether you are a nation or an individual—makes more difference to your income than it ever has before.

This is a critical time for the United States. We have to figure out how to enable the students who now leave school with a 7th or 8th grade reading level and a poor command of 8th grade math (National Center on Education and the Economy, 2013) to graduate instead with much higher skills—both cognitive and noncognitive skills—and we have to figure out how to do it for not much more than we are spending now, because there simply is no more money. We will have to do this at a time when the U.S. economy has turned into two economies: a first-world, high-tech cosmopolitan economy of well-to-do people, and a third-world economy of working and nonworking poor people in which children often grow up without the kind of family support, health care,

---

1. See the reports from the Programme for International Student Assessment (PISA) from the OECD in Paris, France, described and cited in more detail in Chapter 2.

and cultural stimulation that children in the other economy can take for granted (Temin, 2017).

We can hear you saying that the target we just set is impossible. If our schools are having a hard time producing the current level of achievement with the funds now available, how on earth could we reach the nirvana of outcomes that was just painted without spending a whole lot more money, especially given how far behind our students currently are?

We know this can be done because most of the countries that have been outperforming us have been spending less than we do.[2] In this book, we are going to tell you how they did it. We will extract from their experience the core principles that they used to build these systems.

But this is not a recipe book. All countries, indeed all states, are different. They are different in their histories, values, economic systems, mixes of cultural and religious backgrounds, and legal structures. For this reason, instead of giving you scripts to follow, we will give you ideas to use and ways to string together those ideas into effective systems that will enable you to match the achievements of the countries, states, and provinces that now set the global benchmarks.

The phrase "string together those ideas into effective systems" is not a throwaway phrase. It is a key to this book and to the success of the countries with the top-performing education systems. Though the average performance of American students compares very poorly to the average performance of students in the top-performing countries, educators and policymakers from all over the world continue to visit our schools, talk to our leading education thinkers, and study the results of our researchers. Why? Because they are looking for what they call our "peaks of excellence."

---

2. See Chapter 7 for a discussion of this point. Most of these countries spend much more than the United States on support for families with young children, and their budgets for some costs that we include in school budgets are not included in their school budgets. When these costs are accounted for, the United States may not spend more than these other countries do per student, but they *are* showing that much more can be achieved for the same amount of money at no more cost than the United States spends now.

The United States is home to some of the finest schools in the world. Much research that is used to build first-rate education systems elsewhere was conducted in the United States. Many of the world's most influential education thinkers call the United States home. Remarkable things can be found in many schools and districts. Some states have been gaining ground on the top performers, and one is in their league. You can find a terrific example of almost everything somewhere in the United States. There is a lot to build on here and many resources with which to do it, but it is very, very hard to find places where those excellent things are strung together into systems that work for all students. Our peaks of excellence are world-class. Our systems are far from world-class. This book was written to help you build highly effective systems for educating students from a wide range of backgrounds to world-class standards.

What do we mean by a system? Put yourself in Elon Musk's place as he thinks about building the rockets he will use to launch the next phase of space travel (Vance, 2015). Would he consider putting a Briggs and Stratton two-cycle lawnmower motor in his rocket as its power plant? Of course not. He would start by figuring out how much his payload was going to weigh and then how much thrust would be needed for how many minutes to get that payload, the rocket, and the fuel free of Earth's gravity and on its way at the right direction and speed. He would decide whether to use solid fuel or liquid fuel or some combination for the first and second stages of the rocket, based on their weight, burning efficiency, thrust, and so on. Every part and piece of the rocket would have to be designed in detail this way in light of the characteristics of every other part and piece so that, when they are all assembled into a working rocket, the whole thing works perfectly to the specifications with which the designers started. Change one part, one piece, and the engineers will need to figure out what the impact will be on all the others. The whole thing is one integrated system, composed of myriad subsystems. Each part of each subsystem has to be designed with all the other parts of that subsystem in mind. And each subsystem must be designed to work in harness with the other subsystems.

When you think like that, you are thinking like a designer of systems. But that is not the way education policy is made in the United States, nor is it the way our schools and districts work. We live in a world of silver-bullet solutions (NCSL, 2016), and our schools look like a mortuary of silver-bullet solutions, one piled on another in a great heap, except that, unlike in the mortuary, the dead are still alive. Each silver-bullet solution is still being pursued in a school or district somewhere, creating a rocket that cannot fly.

But this is not what we have seen in the top-performing countries. We see carefully designed, complex, and highly effective subsystems for assuring, for example, a steady supply of top-quality teachers, large enough for all their schools, not just a lucky few (Darling-Hammond, Burns et al., 2017). Those systems are just one subsystem among many, integral parts of much larger, carefully designed systems. Among the other parts are subsystems designed to ensure that all children arrive at school ready to learn; that funds available for schooling are distributed fairly among their schools; that instructional systems are set to world-class standards and are coherent and powerful; that expectations are the same for all their students rather than being a function of students' social class or race; that all the students who move between one stage of their schooling and the next are ready for that next stage and not years behind; that their schools are organized and managed not on the old industrial model prevalent in the United States but more along the lines of modern professional service organizations; that schools are led by school leaders who are themselves excellent teachers and who have the skills needed to manage teachers who are treated as real professionals; that teachers are offered real careers and need not have the same job on their last day on the job as they had on the first, and do not have to become principals in order to feed their families; and that career and technical education is no longer a dead-end for students who are not very good at academics but an option for talented youngsters who want a much more applied form of education that is also academically demanding. Each one of these policy arenas is itself a subsystem that has to be designed carefully to reach the objectives their designers have for them. But it is no less true that all need to be designed together so that they work easily and well with each other.

Musk did not just set out to design and build a functioning rocket. He wanted a rocket that would be cheap enough to inaugurate the era of commercial space travel. That meant he needed not just a good design, but a fundamentally different design, one that would get top-notch results for much less money. To get there, he needed, among other things, to have a first-stage rocket that would be reusable, that would float out of space after the launch and then settle down on a barge at sea, right side up, ready to be used again. No one had ever done that before.

To build the rockets he needed, Musk had to go back and rethink everything we thought we knew about how to build a rocket, question every assumption, imagine very different ways of doing things. It is as much a matter of rethinking the principles underlying the way the whole system works as it is thinking about how smoothly the parts and pieces work together.

The United States may be well behind the top performers, but we can turn that to our advantage. In the 19th century, when the United States was just putting together the education system we have now, the Prussians had taken the lead in creating public primary schools, the Germans had created the modern research university, and the Scots were far ahead in vocational education and training. Enterprising Americans went to see what they were doing, brought these ideas back to the United States, and built something even better, on a far greater scale, and ended up in the lead.

Our advantage is simply that we are now in a position, once again, to stand on the shoulders of those who have pioneered the new system. If American ingenuity is still alive and well—and we think it is—then we can once again learn from the leaders. If other countries in many parts of the world can do this, there is no reason we cannot do it at least as well as they have done.

We have used this preface to share the headlines with you, to give you a feel for the shape of the book to come. As you can see, the topics we will cover range widely as we examine what has come to be a worldwide revolution in school design. In the end, this book is about leadership and the role you can play in leading that revolution here at home, with your board, your central office executives, and your principals.

Our aim is to help you understand the principles behind the work of these others so that you can build systems at least as effective as the ones they have built. The school leaders who succeed in bringing U.S. schools into the front ranks of schools worldwide will be the leaders who grasp this agenda, who understand why it is so important to embrace it, and who have the skills needed to design their own systems to successfully implement this agenda. These school leaders will be designing and building the rockets of schooling.

Acknowledgments

Although this book was the product of my fingers flying across my computer keyboard, it was no less the product of a professional lifetime, the last 30 years of which were spent at the National Center on Education and the Economy among colleagues—staff, advisors, and consultants—who contributed in countless important ways to our collective enterprise. The book is, in that sense, the work of a collegium. I am particularly indebted to Betsy Brown Ruzzi and her colleagues at the Center for International Education Benchmarking, whose research has found its way onto every page of this book.

My heartfelt thanks to Robert Rothman, who contributed in many indispensable ways to the production of the book, from helping to think about its organization, to reacting to various versions of the text, to securing permissions, and much more. Brendan Williams-Kief played an important role in coordinating with ASCD. Susan Hills, acquisition editor at ASCD, proved to be an insightful and unfailingly helpful editor.

I am grateful to Vivien Stewart for her extensive comments on the book. I am also grateful to Anthony MacKay and Jack Dale, who commented on the whole book, and for Jason Dougal's and Larry Molinaro's comments on Chapter 8.

1

Systems That Work, Systems That Don't, and No Systems at All

L ooked at one way, the American education system doesn't look like a system at all. Looked at another way, it looks like a system designed to fail. What does a system designed to get better and better look like? Why is it so hard to develop these kinds of healthy, high-performance education systems in the United States? We will explore these questions in this chapter and highlight the crucial role of leadership in designing better systems.

We explained in the Preface that this is a book about building high-performance education systems, and we used Elon Musk's rockets as an example of a high-performance system, pointing to the way that all of the components of his rockets must be designed to work in harmony with all the other parts in order for the rockets to perform to their exacting specifications. In the next chapter, we will help you understand how the top performers have divided their education systems into their component subsystems and the strategic decisions that have driven the design of each of those component systems.

Before we do that, we will help you see how systems work as a whole in education. We want you to get into the habit of "systems thinking." In this chapter, we will show you why we think the "American problem," if you will, is a compound of two problems: collections of components that were never designed to work in harness at all (leaving us, properly speaking, with no system at all) and poorly designed systems that undermine the very purpose for which they were created. To illustrate how our system actually works—or doesn't—we will begin with the story of Harriet Minor. Hers could be the story of any good, experienced, caring teacher in a large school district in many parts of the United States over the past 20 years.

Harriet Minor's Story

Harriet Minor had been teaching at Jefferson Elementary School in Springfield for 15 years. She is a good teacher, highly respected by her colleagues and principal, and a favorite of parents and her students. She enjoys her job and is proud of her accomplishments. But lately she has been thinking about hanging it up and leaving teaching.

Jefferson just got another principal, the fourth in six years. Each one had arrived with a new idea, a new project, a new intervention. The first was convinced that parent involvement was the key to success. The second was a phonics devotee. The third was as far over to the whole-language side of the great reading debate as one could be and was into technology. The fourth thought technology was just a fad. But it wasn't just the principals. One year a couple of teachers who were close to the principal would go to some workshop and come back with a new way to group students, and the principal would shower resources on that method. The next year that program would fall out of favor, but then someone in the central office would become enamored of a new program on data and data analysis. Last year, the superintendent had ordered all the elementary school teachers to attend a workshop series on the new flavor of the month. Those who did not call in sick sat through the workshops, collected their pay, and went back to what they had been doing, secure in the knowledge that this, too, would pass.

All these interventions were laid down one after another by various teachers, principals, central office administrators, and superintendents. None of them were designed to build on what went before, but none of them ever went away, either. They were like the evanescent enthusiasms of teenagers, intense but fleeting and often conflicting.

As Harriet thought about the endless series of silver-bullet solutions that never solved anything, she mused that no one seemed to get any credit for following through on someone else's initiatives. All the kudos seemed to go to the person who came up with a new idea, not the one who put in the work needed to make the old ideas work.

But her school and district, she realized, were now not the only sources of silver-bullet solutions. Harriet had been a teacher for decades, and her mother and grandmother had been teachers before her. Harriet knew that 60 years earlier the federal government had played hardly any role in public education and, at least in her state, the state department of education had little to say about how students were educated in the district schools. In Harriet's grandmother's day, there were no state standards for students, no required state tests or exams, no approved textbooks, no accountability system. There were hardly any requirements for becoming a teacher. The district set its own graduation standards. Most of the money to run the schools was raised by the community and spent in the community. Teachers pretty much decided for themselves what to teach and how to teach it. In most communities, teachers had more education than the average citizen, and they were looked up to. The term *dropout* was unknown, because it was common for most students to leave school when they reached the end of compulsory education, and the basic literacy that most students left with was enough to get a good middle-class job if you were white.

But all of that had begun to change in the 1960s, when President Lyndon Johnson got Congress to pass the big civil rights laws and the Elementary and Secondary Education Act of 1965, which created an expanding set of categorical programs for specific groups of students who had not been served well. The big special education program got its start soon after that, too. The federal government had gotten involved because Congress did not trust state and local governments to do the right thing when it came to civil rights, minorities, special education students, or students from low-income families, so it created wave after wave of programs, each targeted at one of these groups, each with its own funding flows, each with its own regulations and, in many cases, each with its own administrative arm in the district central office and its own funded teachers in the schools, reporting right up this structure through the central office, through the state to the federal government. The state then implemented its own versions of these categorical programs. The district set up its own offices within the central office to administer these programs. Eventually, between them, the state and the federal government paid for more of the school operations in Harriet's community than the local taxpayers did. And with the money, came layer after layer of silver-bullet solutions.

Then, in 2001, Congress, disgusted that it had approved hundreds of billions of dollars in aid to disadvantaged students—with little, it seemed, to show for it—got angry at the teachers and their unions and decided to hold the schools accountable for the performance of the students for whom the money had been given. Schools could be closed, principals cashiered, and teachers fired if the students did not perform. When President Barack Obama took office, many educators thought he might overturn this tough accountability policy and the testing regime on which it was based, but he doubled down on it. Instead of holding the schools accountable, he held the teachers directly accountable, with their jobs on the line if students' performance did not improve at the rate specified by the legislation. In 2010, President Obama's secretary of education in effect pressured the states to adopt the new Common Core State Standards for student achievement for English and mathematics literacy that the Council of Chief State School Officers and the National Governors Association had developed earlier.

Harriet read a lot about the standards and liked them. She thought they were a strong step in the right direction and would help her students develop the critical-thinking skills and reading and writing abilities they would need to be successful. She also liked the emphasis on problem solving and conceptual understanding in mathematics. Though teaching the Common Core would be more difficult than what she had been doing, it embraced what she had always thought was most important in teaching. It was the right thing to do.

But Harriet's positive feelings about the standards evaporated quickly.

The state decided to use the old basic skills tests to assess student progress against the standards, even though the tests were not designed to assess the kinds of achievement that the standards called for. Harriet was livid. She had signed up for the standards because they represented the kind of goals she believed in. But now not only her students' performance but also her own performance would be measured against tests she loathed, ones that focused mainly on memorization of facts and procedures, not at all what she admired in the new standards.

Then Harriet discovered that there was no money to buy new texts and materials, even though the old ones were written before the new standards were released and were virtually useless for helping her students meet the new standards. Even worse, when the textbook publishers rushed new ones into print with little stickers on them saying they were aligned with the new standards, Harriet saw right away that they were just the same old wine in new bottles.

When Harriet asked her principal if the central office would give her and a few other experienced teachers in the school the time they would need to work together to create materials aligned with the new standards, she was told there was no money for that. If any new materials were needed, the teachers would have to create them on their own time.

What Harriet loved about the new standards was their reach, the clear intention of their creators to go for a deep understanding of the material and for the ability to apply that understanding to things that really matter. But it was clear to her that many of her colleagues didn't have that kind of understanding of the subjects they were teaching, nor did they have the skills and knowledge needed to teach those subjects at the level anticipated by the standards' authors. She assumed the state and federal leaders who had created and mandated these standards understood that and would provide the extensive training needed so that teachers could implement them effectively. But, when the inevitable workshops were scheduled to "teach the standards," Harriet discovered that the people delivering the workshops could do no more than explain what was in the standards. The standards might call for students to understand why the rules of arithmetic work the way they do, so that they could grasp algebra when they got to it, but that would never happen, Harriet knew, if their teachers did not understand why those rules work. Now, she realized, those teachers would never understand it, and neither would their students.

By this time, it had become clear to Harriet that the new standards were a very bad joke. When the new accountability plan was announced, Harriet could not believe her ears. The legislation required grade-by-grade testing only in English literacy and mathematics. But all the teachers in her school were supposed to be held accountable for student performance, using the mandated tests. How could that be? Well, the social studies teachers and science teachers and media teachers and even the physical education teachers would be held accountable for the students' performance on the tests of English literacy and mathematics! It might be reasonable to hold the mathematics teachers responsible for students' mathematics achievement, but holding the social studies teachers responsible for mathematics achievement . . . . Harriet was astounded.

That was not the worst of it. Harriet started hearing that some of the most admired teachers in the district, teachers who had won prestigious awards for their teaching, were being fired because their students were not making sufficient progress on the accountability tests. This seemed bizarre to her. But it turned out to be true. These were first-rate teachers who had chosen to work in schools serving the students who needed them the most: students who lived in deep poverty; those who were often homeless or, when not homeless, were being evicted from their homes and moving from school to school every few months; and those who might have one parent in jail and another on drugs. The newspapers were on the accountability bandwagon now and demanding the names of teachers whose students were performing poorly. The tests did not detect the names of the valiant teachers who bailed their students out of jail, found a homeless child a place to stay, or went to bat for the child who had just been beaten up by a gang in a new neighborhood. Nor did the reporters seem to care that the tests that showed a teacher to be a genius one year found the same teacher to be a dud the next.

Harriet could see that the best teachers in the inner-city schools were bailing fast, and she was at a loss for how this sort of accountability system was helping inner-city kids.

The last straw came when her principal demanded that she and the other teachers administer miniversions of the end-of-year basic skills accountability tests at the end of every month to make sure that their students were making enough progress to do well on the end-of-year tests. The principal made it clear that she expected the teachers to study the basic skills tests carefully and make sure their students got plenty of drill and practice on those tests all week, every week. All she seemed to care about was that the students did well on those tests, the same tests that Harriet had always despised. It was not long before the parents discovered what was going on and became outraged at a school that had turned into nothing but a test-prep system.

Well, maybe that was the next-to-last straw. The thing that really caused Harriet to throw in the towel was the way the so-called education reformers were talking about teachers. And about principals, too.

The so-called reformers were fond of pointing out that principals were always giving teachers great evaluations, even when the students' scores on standardized tests were abysmal. This seemed to the so-called reformers to be evidence of collusion to protect incompetents. The way to address this problem, they said, was to bypass the principals and for the system simply to get rid of the teachers whose students performed the worst on the standardized tests. This is what had happened to Harriet's friends, the award-winning teachers in the inner-city schools who were fired.

Harriet had been good friends with the principal of her school for many years, long before she had become principal of this school. She knew that this woman cared deeply about the students and wanted all of them to have the best possible teachers. But she also knew that her inner-city district could not afford to pay what the suburbs paid their teachers. Even worse, whenever her district raised its salaries to get better teachers, the suburbs just raised theirs. When her district managed to develop really skilled teachers, the suburbs always raided them. Her principal did not hand out good evaluations because she was lazy or colluding with anyone. She handed them out because she knew it would be hard to get anyone better, so there was no point in alienating teachers who were going to be on her staff for a long time.

Harriet quit in 2015. Over the preceding 10 years, applications to the teachers colleges in her state had fallen 60 percent, pretty much the average for states in her part of the country. The teachers she knew and admired were telling their own children not to go into teaching. The typical school superintendent in her state was serving just about two and a half years, about the same length of time that the average state commissioner of education was serving. Harriet had heard somewhere that these were the shortest times of tenure that had ever been recorded for people in those positions. It was hard for Harriet to imagine how this was going to end well.

Harriet is an invention. But her experiences and feelings are not. The story just told is actually multiple stories. The first is a parable about the never-ending reform of the American education system conceived of as an endless fusillade of silver-bullet solutions shot at a random selection of targets. The second is about the reform of the American education system as a strangely coherent but self-defeating "vicious circle" of reform that leads inexorably not to high performance but rather to steadily worsening performance. Let's tease out these stories.

Lesson One: Real System Reform Wins Over "Silver Bullet" Reform Every Time

When education reform conceived of as a "fusillade of silver bullets" is compared to education reform conceived of as system reform, real system reform wins, hands down.

Harriet's story begins with a series of principals, each of whom rejected or simply ignored the priorities and strategies embraced by the previous principals and superintendents. None of the leaders were around very long. None of these strategies were systemic. Each of them addressed a particular problem, sometimes the same problems addressed by the previous leaders, sometimes very different ones. Either way, these solutions never produced the breakthrough in student performance that was predicted.

This is not a cynical observation. There is no reason to fault the aims of the succession of leaders or to question their belief that, like the conviction of the multiple divorcee about to marry his or her next spouse, this would be "the one." There are good reasons for the leaders to behave this way. Few believed they stood a chance of changing the system as a whole, even if they believed that only a change in the design of the system as a whole was the way to go. Few had a good model of what such a system might look like, even if they believed they could bring such a thing to life. Few felt they would have much time to establish a strong track record in the job. So, most looked for a package of initiatives that would be "doable" in the time available to them.

This way of looking at the world is reinforced by the characteristic approach to education research in the United States, which is to isolate particular reforms and evaluate particular interventions that can be shown to produce certain statistical effect sizes when used with particular kinds of students under stated conditions. The effect sizes are typically very small but statistically significant.

But the research is done in schools and districts in which many such interventions are being used that were never designed to be used together, in the way that all the parts and pieces of Elon Musk's rockets are designed to work in harmony with each other. As a result, when all the parts and pieces of these systems are in place, many of them simply cancel each other out or just don't support one another. It is often surprising that there is any measurable effect at all. As you will see in Chapter 2, this is not speculation or casual observation. This is true in schools and districts, where we can often see bursts of improvement followed by a regression to the mean. And it is true for the country as a whole. What the record shows is that, despite one wave of "reform" after another, none of the reform is truly systemic. There has been no significant change in the aggregate performance of American high school students for many, many years, despite all the silver bullets. One superintendent we know has described American education reform as a series of "random acts of intervention." That captures the idea nicely.

So, one lesson we can draw about the American education system from Harriet's story is that we do not have a system at all, if a system is defined the way we defined it in the Preface. It is not that we have failed to find the silver bullet that will work. The core lesson from the Elon Musk story is that there is no silver bullet that *can* work.

When the federal and state governments started to play more important roles in school policy, they simply added two more sources of "random acts of intervention." It is not at all unusual for federal, state, and local policies to be at odds, working against one another. This is not an argument against federal and state involvement, nor is it an argument for more local control. The federal and state governments got involved for very good reasons that are still valid. Instead, it is an argument against government at any level engaging in school reform conceived of as an endless series of silver bullets, as random acts of intervention.

This observation raises the question as to what it might mean to apply the Elon Musk example to education. What does "system reform" look like in the countries with high-performing systems? For those of us at the National Center on Education and the Economy (NCEE) who have been benchmarking the countries with the best education systems, our visits have had the character of revelations. People who do this sort of work often say that the biggest benefit for them is to see their own country through new eyes, as if a screen has come down and they see clearly for the first time. That is nowhere truer than in the matter of systems. But don't take our word for it. This is the case in the countries we have been studying for years. Let's take a look now at the systems in these countries, keeping in mind the world we just saw through Harriet's eyes. As you read the descriptions of properly functioning systems, try to recall the corresponding features of the typical American system and note the differences.

These countries have standards that are similar to the Common Core, but they are not just for mathematics and literacy in their native language and not just for a few grades. They cover the whole core curriculum, including history, art, music, technology, the sciences, and the rest of the classic core. The state does not leave it up to the teachers to figure out what the curriculum should look like from scratch. It provides curriculum frameworks and even course syllabi, matched to the standards. It either writes and distributes the textbooks or approves texts that are made by private publishers that are closely aligned to the course syllabi. The tests and exams are not unrelated to the standards; they are intended to be used as end-of-course exams for the state-mandated courses. The whole instructional system is designed as one tightly knit system.

It would never occur to policymakers in these countries to improve teacher quality by getting rid of their worst teachers. It seems obvious to them that if you want the best teachers, you need to offer salaries high enough and working conditions attractive enough to convince the best high school graduates to select teaching over one of the high-status professions. And you have to make sure that the higher education institutions they attend are first rate and have first-rate programs closely aligned with the curriculum used in the schools and with the way those schools are organized. Then, once the graduates of the teacher preparation institutions become teachers, you need to offer them the kinds of careers in teaching that first-rate professionals in other fields have.

Beginning in Chapter 2, we will take you inside the details of how these systems work. The point here is to make sure you understand why systems that are no more than random collections of silver bullets can't work. There is no point in raising teacher pay if you do not do the other things required to attract very high quality candidates to teaching. There is no point in raising the standards to get into teachers colleges if you do not make teaching more attractive as a career. There is no point in raising pay to attract talented young people if you do not restructure the way schools are organized and managed in order to keep them in teaching once they begin it. There is no point in having standards that call for students to master complex skills and sophisticated knowledge if the assessments you use to measure their achievement cannot assess these things. It is unfair for those who run the system to assail school principals for failing to assess their teachers honestly if the people who run the system do nothing to increase the supply of good teachers to take the place of those who are not up to the job.

What we see in the top-performing countries, states, and provinces are well-designed and well-implemented systems in which the foot bone is connected to the ankle bone is connected to the leg bone is connected to the knee bone and so on.

Well-constructed systems are no accident. They are designed. Which means they have designers. The top-performing systems are not all designed in the same way. Nor do all of their subsystems work equally well. That isn't just because they are in countries whose people have different cultures and values. It is also because they have different constitutions, legal systems, and politics. The leaders who framed the key features of their systems faced different obstacles and had different opportunities.

But, despite those differences, all their leaders had more success than most American states at building effective and durable systems.

Lesson Two: Systems Can Be Designed to Get Better and Better

Having a system that is coherent is not enough; some systems spiral upward, producing ever-better results, and others spiral downward, producing steadily poorer results.

There are, in nature, different kinds of systems. Some are stable and some are not. The ones that are not stable don't last very long. Those that are stable can last a long time. That's a good thing if they produce good results, but it's not so good if they produce results that are not so good.

Consider two kinds of systems in the public education arena, one based on a virtuous circle and another on a vicious circle, both of them highly stable.

A virtuous circle can look like this: The system designers figure out how to recruit their teachers from the upper rungs of high school graduates and screen them for their ability to relate to young people and their passion for teaching. They educate them well and train them well in the craft of teaching. They create rewarding careers in teaching for them and offer them incentives for getting better and better at the work. They give them a well-thought-through curriculum to teach and a lot of support to enable them to create first-rate lessons for their students. Their students—no surprise—do very well. The students' success is apparent to parents and the community as a whole. Parents and community members have confidence in their teachers and school leaders and vote for increased spending on the schools when the professionals ask for it, because the professionals have earned their trust. Seeing this, the most promising high school students opt for a career in teaching. The universities get a better quality of applicants going into teaching. They ratchet up their standards for admission to teacher preparation programs. Less-able high school graduates don't even bother applying, and the more able ones apply in greater numbers, in part because teacher education is no longer seen as the program you can get into if you cannot get into a more demanding one. The quality of teachers improves even more. They are able to do an even better job for their students, earning even more trust for the teachers, who are given even more professional autonomy, enabling them to do an even better job, with even less regulation of their work.

That is what NCEE has seen happen in the top-performing countries. It takes time for this virtuous circle to form and gather steam, and we have seen countries go backward when they have abandoned the policies that power this trajectory, but when the policies behind this trajectory are followed, it can be immensely powerful, the cause of an upward trajectory in both achievement and equity that can be truly impressive (Fullan & Quinn, 2015; OECD, 2010).

Then there is the other circle, the vicious one. In this system, the teachers come from the lower stretches of the range of high school graduates who go to college, they are paid well below the average for people with the same amount of education, they go mostly to universities with low entrance requirements, and the requirements for admission to their education programs are no higher than for entering the university in the first place. The result is that the top high school graduates do not often consider teaching as a career, and the public, especially university graduates, look down on teachers and would prefer that their own children go into some other line of work. Because regard for teachers is low, when the students do not perform well, the teachers and the principals, who come from the same background, are the first to be blamed. Policymakers, to public acclaim, get tough on the teachers. The teachers tell their own children not to go into teaching. Young people who might have gone into teaching in the past avoid teaching. Student performance declines as the quality of people going into teaching declines, experienced teachers leave early in discouragement, and the morale of the remaining teachers sinks. As student performance declines, administrators issue more and more mandates, controlling what teachers teach and how they teach it, making the profession even less attractive. The public loses faith in the public schools, and the performance of the whole system declines relentlessly. This is pretty much the condition of many of the schools, districts, and even state education systems in the United States.

When things start to go wrong with national or state education systems, the public and politicians tend to blame the professional educators. They rarely stop to think that poor student performance, skyrocketing costs, and the steadily widening gap between the best and worst performers among the students might be the fault not of the educators but of the system in which they work. This is very hard to see if the only system you know is the one you have always lived in. That is what has happened in the United States.

But if instead of blaming the professional educators for poor system performance, you go looking for high and rising student performance, much more equity, and lower costs outside the United States, you see a very different system. It becomes quite clear that the problem is not the professional educators; it is the system our society has created for them to work in. It was not the professional educators who decided to base the design of our system on cheap, poorly educated teachers, nor was it the professional educators who decided that district central offices should be staffed with ever-growing numbers of people to tell the teachers what to do and how to do it. It wasn't the teachers' unions and the voluminous contracts they created that constrained schools; it was school boards that decided to cede more and more authority to unions when they did not want to raise taxes to give teachers pay increases. It was the legislatures that decided to waive the standards for becoming a teacher in the face of teacher shortages rather than raise teachers' compensation to attract more capable high school graduates into teaching. Everyone is to blame and no one is to blame.

The top-performing countries have made very different choices, and those choices have produced very different results. The challenge for the United States is to start building the kinds of virtuous systems that can lead to ever-better results. But constructing such systems takes more than studying the components of systems that are working well. Your chances of success in designing such systems will be greatly increased if you understand the inner principles behind their construction. That quest begins with what we will call the yin and yang of high-performance systems.

The Yin and Yang of Effective Education Systems: Incentives and Supports

All social systems shape the incentives that operate on the people in them. Some of those incentives are positive, and some are negative. Some are perverse, inclining people to do exactly the opposite of what the system was designed to do. The virtuous circle described earlier was full of positive incentives. The vicious circle was full of negative and even perverse incentives. As you read this book, look for the system features that make for positive incentives, and as you look at your own system, keep looking for the negative and perverse incentives. When you think about how to redesign your system, ask yourself not how to make people do what you tell them to do but rather how to create incentives that will get them to *want* to do what is needed to improve student performance.

Some people think "money" when they hear the word "incentive." But financial gain is only one incentive and often not the most important one. For many people, the satisfaction that comes from helping others is a strong incentive. For others, it might be some combination of the chance to be recognized for outstanding performance by colleagues and friends, the opportunity to gain status in the community, the thrill that comes from learning something hard, or the satisfaction that comes from helping others succeed. Organizations work well when the incentives line up with the organization's mission. It is up to the system designer to design a system in which all the incentives align in the right direction.

Focusing on the Most Important Incentives

There are two sets of incentives that tower in importance over all others as you think about how to design your system. The first set is the incentives for teachers to get continuously better at their work. The second is the incentives for students to do their best. It is crucial to focus on these two groups, because they are the workers in the system. We often think of the teachers as the workers and forget about the students as workers. But if the faculty have strong incentives to do their best and the students are sitting on their hands, not much will happen. That often occurs in American schools, because most of our students have weak incentives to work hard. That is a big mistake that the top-performing countries do not make.

The literature on expertise is clear. It takes about 10 years—or 10,000 hours—of experience to become an expert at almost anything. But 10 years is no guarantee of expertise. One becomes expert only if one is working hard for 10 years to get better and better at the work (Gladwell, 2008).

Estimates of the percentage of teachers who leave teaching within the first five years range from 17 to 50 percent (Ingersoll, 2003; Ingersoll & Perda, 2014), whereas the graduates of professional preparation programs for architects, nurses, attorneys, and other professionals are more likely to stay in their chosen profession. Engineers are twice as likely as teachers to stay in their roles (Ingersoll & Perda, 2014). That means that most people who begin teaching never stay long enough to become experts. Research shows that teachers improve the most early in their careers, with one study finding little evidence that teacher improvement continues after the first three years on the job (Rivkin, Hanushek, & Kain, 2005). One could guess that, given how little support most teachers get when they start out, they are working hard in the first three years to keep their heads above water and then, when they have gotten good enough, they slow, because they have no incentive to get better. They realize that, unlike doctors, engineers, architects, and accountants, they will get no more compensation, status, authority, or responsibility if they are very, very good at the work than if they are just good enough.

A system with a design like this will never develop the kind of expertise it could develop if every teacher in the system had the same kind of expertise that professionals in the high-status professions have. That is an enormous loss, but it is fixable. The top-performing systems have figured out how to create strong incentives for teachers to get better and better at their work. We will show you how they did it.

But Incentives Don't Work Without Support

Incentives are one side of a two-sided coin. Support is the other side. You may have the incentives to accomplish something, but if you don't know how to do it, don't have the time to do it, and don't see how it can be done, you probably won't do it. You need both the incentives and support. Harriet liked the Common Core standards well enough, but neither she nor the other teachers in the school got the training they needed to enable their students to achieve the standards, or the materials they needed to support their students' learning, or the time to work together to develop those materials and practice the new techniques they would need to be successful. One of the most important characteristics of the effective systems we see in the top-performing countries is that the support needed to respond to well-thought-through incentives has been anticipated and provided. We will provide you with lots of examples.

Students Need the Right Incentives and Support, Just Like Teachers

The yin and yang of incentives and supports applies not just to school faculty but also to students. In most American high schools, the students who do not anticipate going to a selective college just drift through school in the accurate belief that they can attend some sort of college if they can get a high school diploma, and all they need to get a diploma is passing grades, which mainly means showing up most of the time. There is no high school diploma in the top-performing countries. There is only a system of qualifications that specify what courses you have to take and the grades you must have to go down any of the available paths to further education or work. Talk to students at most American high schools, and you will find that most of them see high school as a place to socialize with their friends and mark time. That is not what you find in the top-performing countries. There, the students are working hard and purposefully, whatever they plan to do next, because they can see a direct connection between doing well in their courses and the ambitions they have for themselves. Harness the energy and commitment of your teachers and your students, and you have a system that will work. Fail to do that, and nothing will work.

Why It Is So Hard to Develop Effective Systems in the United States

Most observers describe the American system of schooling as decentralized. But that is not accurate. If it were, schools would have more autonomy than their counterparts in the rest of the industrialized world to decide what to teach and how to teach it. Instead, they actually have less freedom than their counterparts.

It would be much more accurate to describe the American system as fractionated. Years ago, most decisions about public schools and schooling were made by local school boards and the educators who worked in the local schools. But, over the past half century, state and federal governments have gotten more involved, with increasing conflict among them and, at the state level, a larger number of independent and often competing centers of policymaking authority. The strong effort of early 20th century reformers to depoliticize public education led to a situation in which the education professionals were widely perceived as controlling the schools. When, in the 1970s, school costs started to rise much faster than inflation, and student performance at the high school level failed to improve (U.S. Department of Education, 2012, 2017b), it became inevitable that the education professionals would be blamed for the growing difference between cost and performance. This happened even though a strong case can be made that providing constant outcomes for students with more money was a victory in a context of growing student poverty and increasingly concentrated poverty among children. In any case, it was this growing gap between cost and achievement that led to the test-based accountability movement, the increasing popularity of market-based alternatives to the traditional public schools, and the rest of the vicious circle we described earlier.

The question is how to get out of this vicious circle. In virtually all of the top-performing countries, the ministry of education would be expected to provide the answer. That is where the buck stops. But there is no institution in the United States comparable to the ministry of education found in most other countries. Instead, there are competing centers of authority that produce a cacophony of voices pulling in different directions.

Building High-Performance School Systems in the United States

The Every Student Succeeds Act provides an opportunity to the states to take back a good deal of the authority to make policy for elementary and secondary education that they lost to the federal government in the first decade of the 21st century. Some will use that authority to create much more effective systems of education than they had in the late 20th century. Others won't.

In an ideal world, states would develop the policies needed to fuel the virtuous circle we described earlier. It would then be up to the districts and the schools to implement those policies. That may happen in a few states. But what do school and district leaders do in states where that doesn't happen?

Can they, without strong support from the state, create much stronger systems, ones that will result in much stronger average student performance while substantially closing the gaps between the top performers and the students who are struggling? NCEE has been working for years in the states and with districts and individual schools. The whole process is certainly easier for the districts and schools when the state, districts, and schools are on the same page, but we have seen schools and districts make real progress on the agenda derived from careful study of the world's top-performing systems, even when they are not on the same page as the state policymakers.

This book is full of ideas about how you can redesign your school or district so that it is no longer a collection of random acts of intervention but instead is a carefully designed system consisting of mutually reinforcing incentives and supports. Such systems (1) attract first-rate teachers and support them as they seek to continually improve and (2) create high expectations for students and provide the support they need to fulfill those expectations.

You may find that laws and regulations make it easier to accomplish your aims, or you may find that they make it more difficult. In our experience, there is no state that makes it impossible to design and implement high-performance systems. That means there is plenty of room within the current system to start building the new one, right where you are. It is not the people who are the problem. It is the system that society has asked them to work in. Change the system, and you will get a very different result. It is up to the leaders of the system at every level to change it.

2

The Architecture of High-Performing
Education Systems: An Overview

When David Kearns became CEO of Xerox in 1982, Xerox was the Google of its day. It had gone from start-up to Fortune 500 membership faster than any company in history. It dominated the copier market. Kearns was sitting on top of the world. Not long after he took on the top job, a team of engineers walked into his office, nervous. They had just returned from Japan. They told Kearns that a small Japanese company none of them had heard of called Ricoh was making copiers with higher quality than Xerox's machines and selling them for less than Xerox's cost of manufacture—that is, before all the costs of engineering, marketing, and sales were factored in. A country best known after World War II as a producer of cheap, low-quality copycat equipment had come from nowhere to beat the United States, the world's leading manufacturing country, at its own game. The engineers urged Kearns to sell Xerox before anyone else found out what Ricoh had done. There was, they said, no way that Xerox could compete with Ricoh or the other Japanese firms that were getting into the copying business. "Nonsense," said Kearns. "The Japanese engineers put their pants on one leg at a time, just the way you do. Get on the next plane back to Japan, figure out how they do it, come back here and figure out how we can do it even better." And they did.

The engineers had been right, though, in thinking this was a life-or-death matter for their company. Many other American companies that did not take the threat that seriously went bankrupt as a consequence, some of them storied names in American manufacturing. The ones that survived did what Xerox did. They went to Japan to understand the revolution in manufacturing that Japan had pioneered and to learn whatever they needed to learn to stand on their shoulders and do it even better.

That was in the early 1980s, and the challenge was in manufacturing. This is now, and the challenge is in education. As serious as the manufacturing challenge was then to the United States, the challenge now in education is far more serious for the country as a whole. Just like Xerox in the early 1980s, the United States stands on the edge of a precipice, challenged by countries that used to be far behind and are now far ahead.

Using PISA as the Global Education Benchmark

Unlike Xerox, we do not have to wait for a team of engineers to burst through the door to know we are in trouble. Education researchers have been doing comparative studies of student performance in the industrialized countries since the 1960s, but it was not until the 1990s that political and education leaders in the United States began to focus on other countries. In 2000, the Organisation for Economic Co-operation and Development (OECD) inaugurated its Programme for International Student Assessment (PISA), now the largest such survey in the world. Every three years, PISA administers a survey of student achievement in reading, mathematics, science, and problem solving to 15-year-olds. The first survey was administered in 32 countries, mostly OECD countries, the world's leading industrial nations (OECD, 2000). In 2015, students in more than 72 countries and economies were assessed, including some countries that are still developing (OECD, 2016b). In

2018, more than 100 countries are committed to participating (OECD, 2017b). PISA not only assesses students, but it also asks many questions of students, school administrators, and others, which makes it possible to relate measures of student achievement and equity to other variables such as cost per student, teacher quality, student immigration status, and class size.

One of the many attractive features of the PISA system is that it asks not how well the student has mastered the curriculum, but rather how well the student is able to use what he or she has learned to solve real-world problems. Though the PISA survey is subject to constraints typical of all measures of this sort, it is the most comprehensive comparative longitudinal measure of student achievement the world has ever had. The countries at the top of the list as this book was being written were Singapore, Japan, Hong Kong, China, Canada, Estonia, South Korea, Finland, Taiwan, the Netherlands, New Zealand, and Germany.

How the United States Stacks Up

U.S. performance is mediocre—but it's not because we've gotten worse. Rather, the others have gotten better. In 2000, the first year the PISA survey was administered, out of 32 countries surveyed, the United States ranked 15th in reading, 19th in mathematics, and 14th in science. In 2015, out of 72 countries surveyed, the United States placed 24th in reading, 41st in mathematics, and 25th in science. The United States' scores in mathematics had dropped 11 points since the previous survey in 2012 (OECD, 2016b). Our analysis shows that the overall difference in average scores between the United States and the top performers is as much as two to three grade levels of achievement.

Apart from the recent drop in mathematics, though, U.S. performance on PISA has been pretty steady (OECD, 2016b). The number of nations doing better than the United States has been growing not because Americans' performance has been declining. Other countries are doing better, and more nations are outperforming us. By comparison, over the four-decade history of the National Assessment of

Educational Progress (NAEP), the average scores for our high school students on the reading and mathematics assessments have not varied by more than a few points (U.S. Department of Education, 2012).

Is Stable Performance Enough?

Should we be proud because we've held the line on performance in the face of rising inequality and poverty among children, or should we be worried because our workforce is now among the worst educated in the industrialized world? In other words, is the glass half full or is it half empty? Should we be glad that we have not slipped or upset because we are not doing better?

Another survey from the OECD gives us some perspective on that question: the Programme for the International Assessment of Adult Competencies (PIAAC). The PIAAC is designed to enable comparisons among the workforces of the advanced industrial nations on the core skills of reading, numeracy, and problem solving in technology-rich environments. The Educational Testing Service (ETS) reanalyzed the data from the latest survey to see how millennials in the U.S. workforce compared to millennials in the workforces of the other countries. Millennials will be the core of our workforce for years to come, and the U.S. economy will depend on them.

The ETS survey showed that Americans ages 16–34 in the PIAAC survey were at the bottom in every category surveyed: reading (only Spain and Italy had lower scores than the United States), numeracy (the United States was last), and problem solving (last, again), demonstrating that we now have one of the worst educated workforces in the industrialized world (Goodman, Sands, & Coley, 2017). We might conclude that the stability in U.S. student performance over the past four decades or so doesn't mean the glass is half full; instead, it looks as though the glass is draining fast.

This may seem like a reasonable verdict, but consider other factors in the bigger picture: In that same 40 or so years, the United States has gone from having the most equal distribution of income in the industrialized world to having the least equitable distribution of income in the industrialized world (Stiglitz, 2012). The income of the average non-supervisory wage earner has declined over that period (Krugman, 2014). Family income rose early in that period as women entered the paid workforce to help their families make ends meet, but then it started to decline again when there were no more women to enter the workforce (U.S. Department of Labor, Bureau of Labor Statistics, n.d.). As factories closed in the face of outsourcing, and advancing automation hit the least educated the hardest, communities all over the United States suffered. As more and more parents were incarcerated in burgeoning prisons, there were fewer parents left to take care of their children. As more and more younger men became unemployed, there was less and less reason for women to marry them and form families (Putnam, 2015). Why would they want another mouth to feed? So there were more and more single parents, the great majority of them poor. As older, mostly white, men lost jobs to outsourcing and automation, many started taking drugs, leading eventually to the opioid epidemic (Murray, 2012). As incomes fell, there were more and more evictions and more and more homeless, especially in the cities (Desmond, 2016). As the cost of health care skyrocketed, more and more of the poor, and their children, simply did without.

While all of this was going on, racial isolation—or, should we say, segregation—and social class isolation in the United States were increasing steadily, which meant that for a growing number of Americans there was and would be no way out, no ladders to climb, no web of relationships that might provide a route to a better future (Sharkey & Graham, 2013).

So how is all this relevant to the glass-half-full/glass-half-empty question? The point is that the country has experienced a wrenching shift from an economy in which all boats are rising to one in which a handful of boats are rising, while most are slowly sinking, with the United States becoming not one economy, but two—in which some cities and a few states are doing very well, while most are increasingly struggling. While these enormous changes have taken place nationwide, the average performance of American schools has held steady (U.S. Department of

Education, 2013). Looked at from this perspective, the glass is not half empty at all. In the face of the mounting catastrophe caused by growing poverty and increasing social and racial isolation in the majority of communities served by our schools, the schools have somehow been able to keep the heads of their students above water.

Stable student performance in such circumstances is an enormous achievement, but it is not enough: it could condemn today's students to lives of increasing misery. If they cannot do the jobs that increasingly intelligent machines can do, at lower cost, they will be unemployable. A large fraction of the jobs that were available to their parents will not be available to them, and few good jobs will be on offer to them unless they are far better educated than their parents (Tucker, 2017).

Learning from Those Who Have Gotten Far Ahead of Us

How do we know that we can greatly raise student performance while closing the big gaps? Because others have shown the way. The question is, how can we greatly improve the performance of students for whom we are responsible and substantially close the gaps? It would be nice if we had a lot more money to do that than we have now, but that money often isn't available. So how can we do it in the real world? We can learn from the countries that have already gone down this path. We can follow in the footsteps of David Kearns's engineers as they retrace their steps to the Japanese copying companies.

It is at this point that many people say, well, sure, but these comparisons are not really valid. Copiers may be the same everywhere, but children, schools, and societies are not. In the United States, for example, we educate everyone, not just the elites, the way they do in other countries. Their cultures are different, and it is their culture—especially the very high value placed on education in the countries with a Confucian culture—that explains their student performance, not the way the schools are organized. Those countries are homogeneous, and ours is diverse. And we have so many poor kids . . . .

I will take a moment here to address each one of these challenges, because if you do not accept my premise, then you are not likely to agree with my conclusions.

We educate everyone, not just the elites. That used to be true, 50 years ago. But it has not been true for a long time. Now, almost all the countries with higher average student performance are graduating more of their students from high school than we are (OECD, 2017a). If any country is educating only its elites, it is the United States, not the top performers.

Their cultures are different. The countries we are comparing the United States to are in Europe, Australasia (meaning New Zealand and Australia), and East Asia, as well as Canada. Those countries have no common culture; indeed, they embrace a wide range of cultures. When most people talk about culture as the big explainer of student performance, they are really talking about Asia. But the reality is that not all Asian countries perform well, and some of today's top Asian performers were at one time among the poorest performers. Many people think that Confucianism explains China's success. But Mao Tse-tung, who thought that Confucianism was holding his country back, forcibly ripped Confucianism from the country during the Cultural Revolution of 1965–1975; his successors had to build a new school system from scratch. Shanghai's success is the result of decisions made in the past 40 years, not the past 2,500 years. Similarly, other high performers, such as Finland and Ontario, Canada, have risen from much lower levels of performance because of changes in policy and practice over the past few decades. It is very hard to make a case on the evidence that culture is the big explainer of superb student performance. What unites the top performers is not some feature of their cultures, but rather the principles that underlie the design of their systems.

Those countries are homogeneous, and ours is diverse. Not so. Canada's largest province, Ontario, among the world's top performers, is home to a larger proportion of residents born outside the country than any state in the United States (Statistics Canada, 2011). Australia, a country almost as diverse as the United States, has generally performed well above the United States (OECD, 2016b). Americans tend to think of northern and western Europe as homogeneous, and that has been true in the past, but over the past several decades, many countries in Europe have become home to large numbers of immigrants from the Eastern Mediterranean, North Africa, and Eastern Europe. In some of those countries, immigrants are struggling in school, but in other countries, such as the United Kingdom, Ireland, and Estonia, they are doing very well (OECD, 2016b).

We have so many poor kids. Despite the previously mentioned misconceptions, there is a lot of truth to the claim that U.S. schools must deal with levels of poverty and racial and social isolation that present great challenges. These challenges are compounded by the fact that we provide less support to families with young children than top-performing countries do. At the same time, the United States spends more per student than these other countries do, offsetting, at least to some extent, the increased cost to the schools of providing services to impoverished students that other agencies of government provide elsewhere (OECD, 2017a).

But there is another way to look at this issue. When we look at Singapore and Shanghai, we are looking at two places that, as recently as the 1960s and 1970s, could only be described as third-world countries. They were destitute. Illiteracy was rampant. Yet today, they top the world's education league tables. When we look at the rates of poverty overall among the nations surveyed by PISA, the United States comes out about in the middle. There are a number of top performers in which poverty among children is high and social class is not as good a predictor of student achievement as it is here, and in many of those countries, students living in poverty have a much better chance of performing in the top quartile of all students than they do in the United States. When we put it all together, we conclude that poverty among children is a serious problem for schools in the United States, but it does not account for our poor student performance relative to the top-performing countries. There are countries in which students are just as poor that are doing considerably better. So, even on this point, there is a lot we can learn from the top performers (OECD, 2017a). We will return to this topic in Chapter 7.

Benchmarking and the Comparative Method

How do we know that if we implement the reforms that the top performers have implemented, we will get the same results? The typical approach to research on innovations in the United States is to use statistical techniques to isolate the effects of a particular innovation on some variable of interest, usually student performance. The form of the innovation is narrowly specified and the researcher works to tell the potential adopter what the effect size is likely to be if the innovation is adopted exactly as specified. That might work if we were talking about techniques for teaching students how to decode an English sentence, but officials who run whole education systems are simply not interested in copying any other system. They know their own context will be different in important ways from the systems the researchers studied. They will have their own politics to deal with. The people of their state will have their own values and aims. They will face challenges the researched country did not face.

Because leaders are not interested in copying anyone, a research model that is designed to specify a model an adopter is supposed to copy whole hog will not work. The decision maker instead wants information that can be used to design that school system's own model, drawing on the experience of a variety of top-performing jurisdictions. That involves, at its best, a creative process in which the system designer puts parts and pieces together, often coming from different systems that he or she thinks will work in harness with each other. The designer knows that the likelihood that those parts and pieces will work well together will increase if the parts and pieces are designed based on common principles. Those parts and pieces will have to be compatible not just with each other but also with the culture, history, and politics of the school system. There will be no implementation unless stakeholders from many corners of the state help shape the design. The state will come up with its own "secret sauce" to add to the parts and pieces that were derived from the study of top-performing systems.

What we have just described is based on the industrial benchmarking approach developed by Xerox and other American manufacturing firms in the 1980s to compete with the Japanese manufacturers. Industrial benchmarking has two key components. The first involves establishing the benchmarks, or specific performances that represent the target for one's own efforts. In the case of Xerox, the benchmarks began with the firms that, in their judgment, using their metrics, were redefining copying. In our case, that would be those systems of education producing the highest average student achievement and the greatest equity.

Once the top performers are identified, the second component of industrial benchmarking is focused on finding the common threads in the strengths they share, as well as their own unique strengths that set them apart. What the Xerox benchmarkers discovered is that different companies are good at different things, even if all of them are high performers compared to their competitors. But, if a whole cluster of companies are demonstrating superior performance, then the strategies they are using may be based on different principles than the ones lower-performing companies' strategies are based on.

So the search for explanations of high-performing systems is a search for the general principles common to all of the top performers and, at the same time, the particular practices in some of the top performers that appear to be especially powerful tools for implementing those principles, so that others can combine best practices across the top performers.

To use this benchmarking approach, the National Center on Education and the Economy uses the PISA rankings to identify the top performers and then looks for the principles that appear to underlie the strategies they use that are not found in lower-performing systems. We look for confirmation of our observations when countries enter or drop out of the ranks of the high performers. If we've got it right, countries that enter the ranks of top performers should be adopting the principles we have identified as drivers of top performance, and countries leaving those ranks should be abandoning those principles. And that is just what we have seen.

But this method goes only so far. The countries that have the best career and technical education systems, or the best early childhood education systems, for example, may or may not line up with the list of countries with the best average performance overall. To get to those lists, we adopt a similar procedure, to the extent that we can get relevant data. That is, we define the outcomes we are looking for at the national, state, or provincial level and then collect the relevant data to identify our targets.

The OECD data are rich and endlessly helpful. But they do not tell the reader what political opportunities and obstacles policymakers faced. To get that information, one has to collect and analyze a lot of data, analyze all manner of other documents, talk with a lot of people who look at the system from many different perspectives, and slowly assemble a very complex picture.

The comparative method lies at the heart of this process. We find out what accounts for high performance in general by comparing the top performers to those whose performance is lower, comparing nations' policies before and after they embrace the hypothesized drivers of top performance, comparing countries' implementation of key drivers, comparing countries with the same outcomes on drivers, and comparing countries with the same drivers on their performance. All along the way, OECD does successive surveys, and countries whose political leadership changes pursue changing policies. All these variations enable us to put our working hypotheses to the test and refine them so that they describe the policies and practices that separate the top performers from the others more reliably over time. In the end, the industrial benchmarking process, applied in this way to the study of education systems, is a compound of quantitative and qualitative analysis.

Based on many years of doing this kind of research all over the world, NCEE has constructed what amounts to a composite picture of the principles that underlie the design of high-performance education systems at the scale of a nation, state, or province. It turns out that the principles on which these systems are based are highly coherent, internally consistent, and powerful.

And so, we come now to the $64 question: what are the top performers doing that the typical state and district in the United States is not? We have distilled our answer into nine building blocks. Bear in mind that, although all of the top performers use all of these strategies, they implement them in different ways and to different degrees. Bear in mind, too, that these findings are tentative. They are a work in progress. They always will be, for this is not an exact science.

The Nine Building Blocks of High-Performance Education Systems

The nine building blocks of world-class education systems are summarized in the sections that follow (Tucker, 2016a).

1. Provide Strong Supports for Children and Their Families Before Students Arrive at School

Almost all of the top-performing countries have robust systems for the support of families with young children that have no parallel in any state in the United States. Singapore, for example, provides a one-time baby bonus of US$5,737 for each of the first two children born and US$7,172 for each additional child born, plus US$2,141 for each child every year after that through childhood. These countries typically provide paid parental leave of four months to a year, universal access to free maternal and child health care, universal access to parental education, home visits, infant and toddler education, and developmental screenings and referrals. This is in addition to free health care for the entire population. Most of these countries provide extensive help with free or heavily subsidized child care. Salaries for child care workers are substantially higher in most of these countries (Kagan, forthcoming), with the result that the quality of child care is higher. All of the top performers provide free or very low cost early childhood education and/

or kindergarten for all 4- and 5-year-olds. Most of these supports and services are not means tested; they are available to all families, not just low-income families (NCEE, 2018).

Remember that this strong system of supports for families with young children is found in countries with smaller disparities in income than in the United States, which means that although average poverty rates among children may be the same, we see greater extremes of poverty in the United States and more concentrated poverty than in some of the top-performing countries (OECDStat, 2017). Because most of these services to families with young children are not means tested, there is no stigma for destitute families to take advantage of them, as there is in the United States. The net result of all this is that poor children in these countries are much less likely than poor children in the United States to come to school sick, in need of dental care, hungry, homeless, abused, or with small vocabularies and limited cultural experience. It is no surprise that countries in which young children come to school healthy, eager to learn, and ready to profit from instruction tend to be countries in which children do well in school.

2. Provide More Resources for At-Risk Students Than for Others

Top-performing countries have made explicit decisions to create systems in which all students are educated to standards formerly reserved only for their elites. To make good on that pledge, these countries recognize that less-advantaged students need more resources than those who come to school with greater advantages. Although the supports just described for preschool children can help level the playing field, top-performing countries know that the field can tilt again toward the advantaged students if they do not continue to provide equitable resources to children from low-income families throughout their school careers.

In every top-performing country, it costs more to educate students with disadvantages than those with advantages. Top-performing countries have structured finance systems to provide additional resources to the schools and the students who need them the most. Most of these systems are variations on what is called "pupil-weighted funding" in the United States. The state or province, not the locality, is usually responsible for raising and distributing the funds for schools, and the money is distributed on a formula that starts with the same base for all students, with weights added for particular categories of need, such as poverty or mother's education level, whether the official language of schooling is spoken at home, immigration status, special education status, and so on. In most U.S. states, school funding is based on property taxes, which means the wealthiest communities generate the most funds per student and can maintain lower tax rates than poorer communities (NCEE, 2018).

Because the wealthiest communities in the United States generate more funds per student than other communities, they get the best teachers and can afford low student–teacher ratios. In contrast, the top-performing countries typically set up their systems so that schools serving mostly disadvantaged students have fewer students per teacher. Some of those countries make sure that their best teachers have strong incentives to work in the schools serving the most disadvantaged students. One way they do that is related to their use of career ladders to structure the work of teachers. It is nearly impossible in some of these countries to ascend the career ladders for teachers and principals without spending considerable time in schools serving very disadvantaged students along the way. Many of these countries also provide a strong incentive to top high school students to go into teaching by paying the total cost of their college and graduate education and training. But they often do so on the condition that these students serve at least five years as a teacher *and* that they spend some of this time in schools serving disadvantaged students.

Schools in the United States that serve high numbers of disadvantaged students typically operate as hubs for the delivery of a wide range of community services to students and their parents. One of the best examples are the Judy Centers in Maryland. Most of the top performers don't do this because the universal provision of these services — such as free health care and dental services—continues into the school years. But even in these cases, the school may provide services for all students and their families that may or may not be provided in most American schools, such as free hot lunches and extended-day programs so that parents who are working full days don't have to worry about what will happen to their children after classes are over.

3. Develop World-Class, Highly Coherent Instructional Systems

Top-performing systems typically have well-developed, highly coherent, and very demanding instructional systems for all students that incorporate student performance standards, curriculum, and assessments, as well as the use of instructional methods appropriate to the goals and standards of instruction.

This is almost the opposite of what Harriet Minor encountered when she fell in love with the Common Core State Standards for mathematics and English literacy (see Chapter 1). In contrast to that experience, the standards in top-performing countries are set high not just for mathematics and language literacy but for all the core subjects. Those standards are used to construct curriculum frameworks. The frameworks are used to construct course syllabi. The syllabi are used to build matching examinations. Teachers are taught in teachers colleges to teach these courses and use these exams. The whole thing fits together seamlessly.

We will discuss instructional systems in considerably more detail in Chapter 4.

4. Create Clear Gateways for Students Through the System, Set to Global Standards, with No Dead Ends

If the purpose of education is to provide students with the knowledge and skills they need to advance to the next stage of their lives, then schools need to provide them with gateways through which they can advance based on what they have accomplished. Top-performing systems do so by awarding students with qualifications, rather than certificates of attendance called high school diplomas, that indicate to postsecondary institutions or employers that they have taken the courses and gotten the grades needed to qualify them to take the next step in their education or their career, depending on their chosen path. Because the state has defined the content of the courses in some detail and the state administers the examinations on which the grades are based, everyone knows just what the qualifications mean, which is not the case in U.S. schools.

These systems open doors; they do not close them. That's because the gateways don't lead to dead ends, as many of our pathways often do. Students change course and move through a different pathway without starting from the beginning. The knowledge and skills they have attained serve as credentials for them on whatever pathway they choose.

We will have more to say about the advantages of qualifications systems in Chapter 4.

5. Ensure an Abundant Supply of Highly Qualified Teachers

It is often—and accurately—said that no education system can be stronger than the quality of its teachers. That is why the top-performing systems place a high priority on attracting and preparing well-qualified individuals to teach so that all students can have access to excellent instruction every day.

In these systems, teaching is an attractive and prestigious profession that well-qualified individuals want to join and that enables the top-performing systems to be highly selective in choosing the most capable and committed high school and college students for teacher education. The preparation programs are rigorous with respect to mastery of the content they will teach and the craft of teaching itself. Despite the high standards that applicant for slots in the teacher education system must meet, most of the top performers have a surplus of first-rate teachers (NCEE, 2018). They never lower their standards for their teachers and do not allow anyone to teach without meeting those standards, which means, among other things, that they do not have what we call alternative routes into teaching.

We will discuss teacher quality in much greater detail in Chapter 5.

6. Redesign Schools to Be Places in Which Teachers Will Be Treated as Professionals, with Incentives and Support to Continuously Improve Their Professional Practice and the Performance of Their Students

The top-performing countries attract many of their best high school students into teaching in part by offering compensation that is competitive with the high-status occupations, whereas salaries for teachers in the United States typically lag far behind those in the high-status occupations and in some states are simply not enough to support a family above the poverty line. But competitive compensation is not the only draw (OECD, 2017a). These countries are redesigning the occupation of teaching and the conditions under which teachers do their jobs in order to attract high-quality candidates as well as to keep them in teaching much longer than the typical teacher. The cost of the current rate of attrition is very high; cutting that cost by half or two-thirds would make it possible to have much higher quality teachers at no greater cost (Learning Policy Institute, 2017).

The changes these countries are making include the construction of a real career in teaching that mimics in its design the kinds of career progressions that attorneys, engineers, and accountants have, so that young people can look forward to staying in teaching as their career matures and they gain responsibility, authority, status, and pay as they move toward the position of master teacher.

But that is not all. The top performers are also reorganizing the school to change what it means to be a teacher. Much less time is spent teaching, and much more time is spent tutoring students who need intensive assistance and working on teams with other teachers to steadily improve every aspect of the school's program, including the curriculum, the courses, pedagogy, and assessment. Teachers actually have office space and a lot more time to work together. They conduct action research and publish their findings in refereed journals. They mentor newcomers and have time to visit schools in other districts, states, and even countries.

Put it all together, and you will see that these top-performing countries are creating a whole new profession of teaching, one that looks a lot more like the high-status professions in the United States. We will tell you how they are doing this in Chapter 6.

7. Create an Effective System of Career and Technical Education and Training

In no advanced industrial nation do a majority of high school students go on to earn university degrees. That means that the majority of the members of their workforces have less than a bachelor's degree (OECD, 2017a). The economies of the advanced industrial countries depend heavily on having a highly trained, and very large, core of technical workers who can do most of the work. The demands on this "middle-skill-level" workforce are ratcheting up very quickly as low-skill jobs migrate to countries that charge much less for their labor and automation takes an increasing number of the low- and middle-skill jobs that are left.

In the United States, and some of the countries with high academic performance, vocational education is what you pursue if you cannot pursue academics. But that is not true in a growing number of advanced industrial countries that have seen the high-skill future coming. Those countries have been busy redesigning their vocational education and training (VET) systems so that the curriculum for VET courses assumes a high level of academic mastery, just like the courses designed to prepare students for university. All students are expected to master that high academic standard by the end of their sophomore year in high school, no matter what they want to do after that. Those who choose VET for their junior- and senior-year programs are preparing either to take industry-approved examinations at the end of their senior year that qualify them to begin a rewarding career or to obtain a qualification that will enable them to attend a demanding program in a VET postsecondary institution, like a polytechnic in Singapore or an applied university in Switzerland.

These VET programs, unlike the typical experience for an American high school student enrolled in a career and technical education program at the high school level, typically involve serious apprenticeships—not internships—in firms that must meet stringent requirements before they gain the right to offer an apprenticeship. Apprentices learn their trades or occupations on state-of-the-art equipment from instructors who complete regular tours of duty in state-of-the-art settings, to ensure that they are keeping up with advances in their respective fields. Students train to demanding standards established by industry groups, and apprentices work for wages lower than the prevailing wage in a system established and monitored by the government.

Pieces of a system like this can be found in the United States, but the system itself cannot. Singapore and Switzerland are the world leaders, but a growing number of countries are trying to catch up to them.

It has not always been this way in Singapore. Just a few years ago, vocational education, as in much of the United States, was widely regarded as a dead end for students who had run out of alternatives.

In 1992, Singapore created the Institute of Technical Education (ITE), which was intended to revolutionize VET and be a world-class example of how vocational and technical skills could be redesigned for a knowledge-based economy. The whole VET system was consolidated at four campuses, each newly constructed to have all the amenities of well-funded universities, as well as state-of-the-art technical facilities and a world-class set of industry partners (including, for example, the Rolls-Royce company for commercial jet engine maintenance and repair and Institut Paul Bocuse, a famous French cooking school, for its culinary school). The government created a whole new approach to vocational education, which they branded as "hands-on, minds-on, hearts-on" education to combat the perception that these schools were for low achievers. Since 1995, enrollment in VET has doubled, and the ITE has gained a strong reputation for producing highly skilled workers. In 2014, 87 percent of ITE graduates were hired in their fields within six months of graduation, and salaries are high (Singapore Academy of Corporate Management, 2014).

8. Create a Leadership Development System That Develops Leaders at All Levels to Manage Such Systems Effectively

It may be impossible to find a really good school with a poor leader. Top-performing systems understand that school leadership is the key to consistently effective schools. High-quality leaders attract and support high-quality teachers and provide them with the resources and tools they need to improve their practice continually. To ensure a steady supply of effective leaders, top-performing systems do not wait for individuals to apply to become leaders. Rather, they identify promising candidates from the ranks of effective teachers, groom them over a period of years, and give them progressively more demanding opportunities to lead their colleagues as a teacher, as well as other opportunities to build their leadership skills and knowledge, including having a chance to work with a skilled mentor.

Just as running highly effective school districts requires a very different kind of district design than is typically found in the United States, the same thing is true of schools. They, too, require a different kind of design. We briefly summarized some characteristics of the new design earlier in this chapter. It is up to the principal to implement the design and to make it work well.

To do so, the principal must have a very different set of skills than the typical American school principal. There is a real premium on being able to manage *professionals*, as that word is defined in environments employing high-status professionals. Most central office staff in American school districts define a good principal as one who carries out the directives put out by the central office and who does not create the kinds of problems central office staff would rather not deal with. Most teachers define a good school principal as one who is adept at getting resources out of the central office.

In the modern design, by contrast, a good principal is one who can establish a vision for a high-performance system that will capture the imagination of parents, students, faculty, and the community; who will involve everyone in creating a design for the school that will reflect the vision and lead to its realization; and who will develop effective strategies for implementing the design. This is principal as architect and builder. But the materials are all human, which means the principal must over time hire and carefully place the key staff he or she will need to transform the school, redesign the master schedule to find much more time for those teachers to redesign the curriculum, create the courses, develop the new assessment techniques, and do all the other things required to greatly improve the performance of the school and its students.

The changes needed in school leadership will require a lot of planning and preparation. In Ontario, the ministry of education created an extensive Ontario Leadership Strategy, a comprehensive plan of action designed to support student achievement and well-being by attracting and developing skilled and passionate school and system leaders. Under the strategy, the ministry provides local school boards with funding and support to enable them to recruit strong individuals into leadership positions; to place those individuals to ensure sustained school and system improvement; to develop them through high-quality, research-based preparation programs, performance appraisal, and learning opportunities; and to support them by providing them with information and buffering them from distractions.

We will have something to say in Chapter 8 about how leaders can drive the design and development of the entire high-performance system described in this book.

9. Institute a Governance System That Has the Authority and Legitimacy to Develop Coherent, Powerful Policies and Is Capable of Implementing Them at Scale

Effective systems work when their policies are coherent and consistent, and when they are enacted and implemented consistently throughout the system. When NCEE visits the top-performing countries, we always ask the people in the ministry of education a set of questions about key policies and practices and then ask the same questions of officials, teachers, and observers at every other level of the system. When we are in a top-performing system, virtually everyone we talk with describes the system in pretty much the same way.

But when we are in the United States, that is very, very unlikely to happen. People in different roles and at different levels of the system understand the priorities and substance of policies very differently, and their views about what needs to be done and how it is to be done conflict substantially with one another. Many different agencies, bureaus, commissions, departments, and institutions, all of which have official roles, proceed more or less independently of one another and often in quite different directions. One would not expect much coherence in policy or practice in such an environment, and indeed we do not often see much coherence.

But there are ways to ameliorate this kind of chaos. In Ontario and Singapore, for example, the ministry of education arranges for teachers to spend part of their career in the ministry. The teachers provide input into policymaking based on their experience, and when they return to the classroom, they help translate the policies to their peers. Much the same thing could be done by giving school teachers tours of duty in the central office and district central office executives tours of duty in state departments of education, which might help the inhabitants of these various domains better understand the points of view and imperatives of the people for whom they are making policy or, if they are people for whom it is being made, the points of view of those who are making it. This modest innovation might contribute a great deal to increasing the coherence of the whole system.

In the long haul, however, what we at NCEE see is that, as the quality of school staff increases and as that high-quality staff earns more responsibility and more autonomy, the need for staff above and around them declines. School staff accounts for more and more of the total budget and the number of staff needed to govern the system, manage it, and provide specialized services declines. That process releases funds that can be used to raise teacher compensation, which will attract even more competent teachers. Student performance improves. The public has more confidence in the education professionals. And things get even better. The virtuous circle emerges from the shadows to replace the vicious circle. Student performance, equity, and efficiency just get better and better.

The System as More Than the Sum of Its Parts

The most important characteristic of the nine building blocks is not the details that lie behind this brief summary, but what we at NCEE call their "systemness." That is a reference to the fact that they constitute *one* system, not nine independent systems. As we said earlier, if the state limited the right to offer teacher education and training to its top universities but did nothing to make teaching more attractive, the supply of young people interested in going into teaching would dry up. If it raised compensation but continued to get its teachers from the lower reaches of its high school graduating classes, it would be wasting its money. If it gave its teachers strong research skills but provided its teachers no time to use them, the investment in research skills would be wasted. If it improved teacher quality, but did nothing to improve school leadership, great teachers disgusted with poor leadership would change professions. The examples are endless. The point is that the top-performing nations, states, and provinces get the results they get by thinking very carefully about how all these parts and pieces should fit together. They do not build them all at once, but they do keep the whole thing in mind as they design their building. They think like architects.

You might have expected us at this point to take the building blocks one by one and tell you how the top performers approach each of them and how we think you can use that information. If we were we writing for state policymakers, we would do exactly that, but we are not. In the rest of this book, we are going to concentrate on those aspects of the nine building blocks that are most directly under the control of district and school leaders, addressing the other building blocks in that context when they are relevant.

Along the way, you will see sidebars containing material from interviews we have done with chief state school officers, school superintendents, and others whom we asked to talk about work they have done or are doing that is directly related to the strategies used by the top performers. We are confident that you will find both encouragement and some good ideas in these stories.

3

It Begins with a Vision
That Becomes a Plan

How does a district turn the incoherent nonsystem that Harriet Minor experienced into a coherent system that incorporates the nine building blocks of effective systems described in Chapter 2? It begins with a vision.

By vision, we don't mean the kind of generic "vision statement" that many school districts and schools have adopted. These vision statements often express universal goals for children that few can dispute but no one expects to be acted on. They are mostly intended to make people feel good.

The kind of vision we have in mind is very different. It is a vision intended as the basis of action, mobilizing a wide range of actors precisely because it embodies their hopes and, at the same time, can be achieved. It has to be a vision that becomes a plan with widespread support that will endure.

A Vision That Can Mobilize
Your Stakeholders

Most vision statements talk about things like students reaching their potential. The faculty and parents who read them assume that, whatever the lofty sentiments expressed in the vision statement, the schools will in the future look a lot like the ones to which they have grown accustomed. That is fine with them, because—as Gallup polls have shown for years—most Americans think their schools are doing pretty well. They think there are big problems in American schooling, but they think the problems are in inner-city schools, not in the schools in their own communities. As long as that kind of thinking holds sway, it will be impossible for school leaders to make the kinds of changes needed to match the achievements of the top-performing countries.

Americans believe their schools are doing pretty well because they are comparing them to the schools they went to themselves. No one has explained to them that that is the wrong way to look at it. The question is not how well the schools are doing compared to how well they used to; it is how well the schools are doing compared to how well they have to now. As we explained earlier, the changes wrought by globalization and the changes about to be caused by advancing intelligent machines are making obsolete the kinds of jobs that most high school graduates have been prepared to do and are greatly changing the demands that will be made on workers and citizens at all levels.

The school leader's first job is to understand these changes and then to help his or her community understand them. School leaders not only need to convey accurately the extent of the threat that students and the community face if expectations for students are not raised, but they also need to convey a sense of hope, the belief that those challenges can be met.

People will not substantially change the core institutions in their communities unless they come to believe that the price of not changing them is greater than the price of doing so.

How Advancing Technology Is Transforming the World in Which Our Students Will Live and Work

Technological change is not new. It was a big issue in England in the early days of the industrial revolution when hand weavers were replaced by power looms. Eventually, as we all now know, the former weavers went to work in the factories. Later, highly skilled machinists were replaced by mass production of interchangeable parts. Agricultural workers were replaced by sophisticated farm machinery. And all of these workers eventually found a place in economies using more and more advanced technologies, each one of them made more productive by the use of that technology than their predecessors had been without it. The productivity increase did not come from more skilled workers. Most of the skills needed to do these jobs and almost all of the muscle power was built into the machines. Most of the work that became available could still be done by people with not much more than what we now think of as the "basic skills" (*The Economist*, 2016).

Many people now say that the same thing will happen this time. New jobs will spring up as the old ones die, and there will be plenty of jobs for everyone, though many of them will be new kinds of jobs we cannot even imagine today. But many observers point to evidence that this time is likely to be different because these machines are "machines who think" (McCorduck, 2004).

We pointed out in the Preface that such advances began to enter the American workforce years ago, with innovations like pumps at gas stations that automated both the pumping and the billing process, point-of-sale registers, self-checkout in stores, and automatic toll takers. More than three decades ago, at the Toyota factories in Japan, robots took giant rolls of steel and fed them into giant presses from which emerged fenders, trunks, and hoods of cars, which another set of robots then painted. Robots welded the frames together and sent them down an assembly line, where other robots attached the parts to the frame.

The robots at Toyota were just the beginning. It is not true that U.S. manufacturing is dead due to offshoring. It is alive and well, but, because of advances in factory automation, manufacturing employment in the United States is a small fraction of what it used to be. Those jobs will never come back, because machines can do them faster, more accurately, more reliably, and cheaper than human beings can. Many industries continue to do well, but the people who used to work in them are not. Much more is being produced by many fewer people, and those people are far better educated and skilled than the people looking for work.

As important as the spread of factory automation and the use of all kinds of productivity software have been, they are only the tip of the iceberg, a foreshadowing of what is coming. It now looks increasingly likely that intelligent technology, driven by advances in artificial intelligence, neural networks, robotics, and machine learning, is likely to have a transformative effect on the world of work in the United States (Tucker, 2017). In the early stages of the application of computers to the kinds of tasks described earlier, the machines were used to do jobs that involved following rules encoded in the software, enabling machines to do certain rule-based tasks, such as calculate insurance premiums, automatically charge your credit card account, or paint car doors at Toyota. Eventually, this kind of intelligent machinery astounded the world when an IBM computer, Big Blue, beat world chess champion Garry Kasparov. There was a lot of talk then about computers taking over all kinds of jobs.

But wiser heads pointed out that 6-month-old children were, on the whole, much smarter than Big Blue. They can pick out the big yellow box, recognize their mother, get a toy, and figure out how it works. Big Blue could not do any of these things. Chess is a game with rules. To win at chess, you have to know the rules and get very good at anticipating what will happen when you and your opponent execute a whole series of moves. That is what these machines were exceptionally good at, which is why the machine could beat Garry Kasparov by what might be called brute force computing. It had simply figured out all the possible game-ending moves for Kasparov and itself very quickly, something that no human could have done. But there is a lot more to human intelligence than that.

It turns out, however, that many jobs human beings get paid to do require the same kind of rule-following that these computers can do. If your work requires little more than middle school literacy and middle school mathematics and mainly involves following routines that can be incorporated in software, the chances are good that your job can be done more cheaply and more reliably by an intelligent machine.

That point was made for many educators in *The New Division of Labor: How Computers Are Creating the Next Job Market* (Levy & Murnane, 2004). Frank Levy and Richard Murnane warn educators that the ability of computers to do an ever-widening array of jobs involving routine work would eventually render large numbers of high school graduates unemployable or employable only at much lower wages. Some jobs involving routine work would disappear altogether, like the buggy whip maker of old. Others, like secretaries, would be transformed into jobs requiring much more education because intelligent machines could not do the cognitive work involved, like research on the Internet, training others, coordinating complex operations, and so on (Levy & Murnane, 2004).

They contrasted the jobs involving routine work with another kind of job, jobs that involved cognitive work that the machines would not be able to do. The example they chose was making a left-hand turn in traffic. It was obvious then that the machines could not recognize all the objects—moving and stationary—that a driver has to take account of, anticipate what other drivers and pedestrians are likely to do, and instantly adjust driving strategy when the unexpected happens. Levy and Murnane guessed that it would be a long time, if ever, before intelligent machines would be able to do what human drivers routinely do.

The New Division of Labor was published in 2004. Six years later, automated cars designed and owned by Google were driving down Highway 101 in Los Angeles, with no one at the wheel.

Just one year after that, in 2011, IBM's Watson computer won in a game of *Jeopardy!* against champs Ken Jennings and Brad Rutter. To get there, a team of 20 IBM researchers and software developers had to develop a computer that would understand the kind of language that people use in everyday life, with all its ambiguity, fuzziness, humor, and irony. An IBM document written at the time to convey the nature of the challenge pointed out, "We have noses that run, and feet that smell. How can a slim chance and a fat chance be the same, but a wise man and wise guy be opposites? How can a house burn up as it burns down?" (Ford, 2015). To do this, developers found a way to break the challenge down into all its component parts and then create algorithms that would enable the machine to solve for each part. The algorithms enabled the machine not only to look for answers but also to rank the answers according to the probability that they were right. In the process, IBM had gotten a lot closer to a machine that could think the way human beings think. This was a big step beyond brute-force computing.[1]

The IBM team had made extensive use of research done by cognitive scientists, who found that children learn by developing theories and testing them in rounds of trial and error, which provided the foundation for machine learning. Today's machines can go beyond achieving a goal with the help of rules to get them there; now what they need is the goal and access to a great deal of data in order to try out ideas on the data until they can learn what they need to learn to accomplish the goal.

In 2016, a Google computer did something that appeared to be similar to the chess win for Big Blue years earlier, but in fact was very different. It beat a world champion at the game of Go, an ancient Chinese board game. The difference is that an almost infinite number of possible moves are available to a Go player. Brute-force computing won't work. Go players win by recognizing patterns on the board that open up some options and close others. After years of experience, a kind of intuition takes over. It is this intuitive capacity that the Google programmers had captured. The Google machine had inferred the answers with a kind of intuitive approach based on patterns. It turns out that a great deal of human thinking works this way. It was a giant advance (Sang-Hun & Markoff, 2016).

Software that has something that might reasonably be called intuition, combined with software that enables intelligent machines not just to execute preestablished routines but to learn in much the same way

---

1. This story is well told in Martin Ford's *Rise of the Robots*.

that humans learn, combined with access to networks and servers loaded with unimaginably large bodies of data, have changed the whole game.

What does all this mean for the kind of skills and abilities that today's kindergarteners will need as adults? Experts differ widely on the answer to that question. Some believe that intelligent agents will put the majority of human beings out of work because most of the work that will be needed will be done by machines that can do it cheaper and more reliably than human beings will be willing to do the work for (Ford, 2015). Some believe that the problem is not too much intelligent technology but too little (Swanson & Mandel, 2017). Some believe that the machines will take over and humans will become their slaves (Harari, 2017). Others believe that machines will do all the work that humans do not want to do and intelligent agents will usher in a sort of utopia in which human beings will be free to enjoy themselves and develop their potential to the fullest (Kurzweil, 2005).

The truth is that plausible arguments can be made for all of these futures. What is striking, however, is that virtually all of these experts say that most of the work that will be available and will enable workers to support themselves above the poverty level will require much higher and more diverse skills from our high school graduates than they currently have.

That is because much of the work requiring what we think of as only the basic skills is the work that is easiest for the machines to do and the first to go. Most manufacturing, mining, retail, and driving jobs (driving cars, trucks, limos, and buses) are under threat as this is written. Note that the industries just named now employ a very large number of Americans.

While all this is going on, the job market is changing fast. Whenever there is a downturn, companies are investing in more intelligent machines, so that they need fewer humans when business picks back up. There is a fierce bidding war among companies for the handful of people who can invent the future using intelligent agents of all kinds. But there is a vast and growing surplus of poorly educated labor. Because there are more people with low skills than the market can absorb, their wages are slowly sinking. Bigger companies are cutting back their permanent full-time, benefit-earning staff and using more and more "independent contractors" to whom they do not have to pay benefits and whom they can hire only when they need them. That is increasing the number of workers in the so-called "gig economy" who often contract with multiple companies at any one time, often doing very different things for different companies. This is a world in which there is much less loyalty between companies and employees. One consequence of this is that employers are much less willing to invest in the education and training of their employees than they used to be, because they know that workers can take the new skills to a competitor if the opportunity arises. A large part of the workforce will be working, but not in steady jobs. Rather, they will likely be independent entrepreneurs continually finding new clients and learning whatever they have to in order to get the next job.

Many companies and analysts are thinking about the advances in intelligent agents as complementing the skills that humans bring to the workplace (Manyika et al., 2017). Rather than asking which jobs will be done by the machines, they are asking which parts of which jobs now done by human beings will be done by machines and, therefore, what parts of those jobs will be left to be done by humans. This idea lives side by side with the fact that the new technologies are often not just changing the nature of existing jobs but are wiping out entire industries (Ford, 2015). This means that people employed in regular full-time jobs with benefits will have to live with the reality that their industry could be wiped out or their jobs could be redefined.

The Bottom Line: What Your Students Will Have to Know and Be Able to Do in the New Economy

Where does all this leave educators who need to understand what kind of world graduates of their schools are likely to be living in two or three decades from now?

1. *Students who leave high school with only the levels of literacy and skills that most high school students now leave high school with will be in deep trouble.* Not only will they lack the education and skills needed to do the work for which employers will pay enough to support a family, but they will be so far behind that it will appear to them that there is no way to catch up as an adult.

2. Because most employers will expect candidates for jobs to be ready to do them, your students will have to be job-ready with considerable technical competence to get their first jobs, whether they apply for that job from high school or from college. *You need to make sure that your graduates have a credential when they leave high school and that credential will have to certify that the individual either is ready to go to college without remediation or has all the skills needed to be hired for an entry-level position that pays reasonably well and leads to a career that will enable that person to support a family.* Only approximately one-quarter of high school students leave high school with such a credential now (U.S. Department of Education, 2017a). This implies an enormous ratcheting up of the current high-school-leaving standard.

3. Because there is a very high likelihood that your graduates will be making many significant career changes with increasing frequency and, in fact, working several different and changing careers at once, *you need to make sure you have given those graduates the skills needed to learn complex things very quickly and easily.* Just as the last point implied that graduates will have to be very well trained or ready for high-level training, this point implies that those same graduates will have to be highly educated, with a much deeper understanding of the core subjects in the curriculum than high school graduates have now and that they will need the ability to apply that understanding to a wide range of practical problems. That will require real mastery of the underlying concepts, strong analytical skills, equally strong skills of synthesis, and very strong communications and just plain thinking skills.

4. Because your graduates will likely, at some point in their careers, be working for themselves and taking on a changing array of clients, *they will have to be very disciplined, able to set a goal for themselves and organize themselves to achieve it on time and to the needed standard, and able to juggle a changing array of challenges all at the same time.* If they tend to wait around to be told what to do and how to do it, they will have a rough time. They will need to be able to communicate well with their clients and with a wide variety of people whose services they will need in order to deliver what their clients want when they want it.

5. *Communications skills will be paramount,* whether an individual works alone as an independent entrepreneur or as a member of a team as a full-time employee in a firm. Your graduates will have to be able to make reports, create plans, sell their services, request services, deliver instructions, and analyze options for others all day every day in clear, concise language.

6. *Because intelligent agents will do more and more of what has to be done, humans will have to get better and better at what is left, if they are to have work. That means, in essence, that humans will have to get better and better at what is essentially human.* It will be a while, if ever, before intelligent agents can inspire, lead, comfort, love, display courage, show empathy, be tolerant, provide solace, be a great team member or colleague, create a new industry, figure out a winning political strategy, design a whole new way to think about what furniture should look like, take the intellectual leap that results in a whole new theory of the fundamental physics of the universe, create a new style of music, or give a student a reason to reach for the stars. Schools will have to be redesigned not to focus largely on the kind of cognitive development that our classrooms now favor, but to include as equally important development of all the qualities just mentioned and many others like them.

7. *Perhaps most important, your students will need a very well grounded set of values.* This may be the most important human

attribute of all. Intelligent agents do not know right from wrong and do not care. What has truly frightened many people who are deeply versed in the world of intelligent agents is the prospect of immensely powerful but totally amoral machines. If developments continue on their current path, these machines may well lead to a world in which there will be a handful of immensely powerful and very rich people and a far larger group who are just getting by. Some insiders, including Bill Gates, worry that some of these machines could, in their single-minded pursuit of some goal, take over from human beings and turn us into pets or worse (Holley, 2015). Others see almost the opposite, a world in which intelligent machines create a world of unimaginable comfort and fulfillment for all humanity (Kurzweil, 2005). Still others see their use leading to the demise of democracy in a world in which a handful of oligarchs keep the public happy with the equivalent of Roman bread and circuses (Harari, 2017). It could be that the most important function of schooling in the years ahead will be the education of an electorate that is able to steer us all through this thicket of possibilities to a world in which all of us and not just a tiny minority benefit from the application of these powerful technologies.

8. The world is far more connected than ever before. Your underwear may come from Bangladesh and your television set from South Korea. The radiologist's report on your aching hip may have come from a radiologist in India. Your son may be on his way to work in the London affiliate of an American bank. We cannot tackle the carbon problem without the cooperation of Indonesia and India. The rare metals used to make your cellphone work probably come from China. The terrorist attack that most worried American officials last week may have been thwarted by intelligence from Israel or Saudi Arabia. Your daughter, working for a high-tech company in Austin, may have teammates in Estonia who use the Internet to participate. Fifty years ago, few of these statements would have been true. Today,

all could be. *Much will depend on Americans' understanding of the peoples of the world and their aspirations, history, values, cultures, grievances, and points of view.*

9. Finally, there is the matter of the Enlightenment values on which the American nation and its constitution are based: the primacy of empirical facts and reasoning as drivers of human progress, the rights of the individual against the government, the role of the press and the courts in restraining the unbridled power of the legislature and the executive, and the need for public participation in the democratic process to make it work. The news that only a minority of young people in the United States now view democracy as important should strike fear into the heart of every citizen of this country, as should the news that there are facts and alternative facts, each with equal standing. *It is important for our young people to begin adult life with the skills they will need to make a good living, but it is no less important that they understand the fragility of democracy and how important it is to preserve and defend it.*

This is not intended to be a full list of the challenges posed by the possibilities inherent in the technologies now under development and by other developments no less significant. It is intended to help you and your stakeholders think about what you want for your young people. We take the position that the future will be discontinuous from the past, not a smooth extension of it; therefore, we need to think differently about what these changes might mean for our young people and schools.

Turning Goals into Plans

It is critical to take many stakeholders in your community along with you on the journey of rethinking goals for the times we live in. The whole point of rethinking your goals is to come up with a plan of action, and the whole point of a plan of action is to have strategies agreed upon and owned by all the people who will have to be engaged in order to implement the plan and achieve the goals. The question is how to go about planning in a way that will lead to broad commitment to that plan.

An important component of such a process is a compelling analysis of the situation your community faces, one that your constituents will recognize as their reality. Beyond that, you will need to outline for your community an appealing and feasible direction to reach your goals for your school. Having a compelling vision is not enough because without a realistic bridge to that vision, your stakeholders will stay right where they are. In this book, much of the strategy we propose to build a bridge to the future comes from strategies other countries have used to achieve a vision much like the one we just shared with you. The enormous advantage of that set of strategies is that we know they work.

The key is to develop a plan for adapting these strategies to the needs of your community and stakeholders. The stakeholders who will agree to the plan and to be responsible for implementing it will have to own it. It is no small thing to conceive and manage a process that will do all this while preserving the integrity of your vision for a powerful, coherent system that gets results.

Planning in Shanghai: An Unusual Model

We want to share with you one example of a process that did exactly that. It is the planning process used by the Shanghai Municipal Education Commission to propel Shanghai to the top of the OECD-PISA league tables years later.

Shanghai first participated in the PISA surveys in 2009, when it topped the charts in all three subject areas. It then repeated that performance in the 2012 results. Not only was Shanghai at the top of the charts, but it had the smallest percentage of students performing in the lowest levels and the highest percentage of students performing at the highest levels of any participating country (OECD, 2014a).

Shanghai's educational success is particularly noteworthy, considering that the city had no education system at all in 1978, when Deng

Xiaoping took the reins in China. It had been destroyed by Mao during the Cultural Revolution. The system was built from scratch and now must accommodate a huge and growing population—today, about 24 million people, approximately 9 million of whom are migrants, most arriving very poorly educated, many speaking a dialect of Chinese unlike the one spoken in Shanghai.

Shanghai's rapid rise and high performance occurred largely thanks to the Shanghai Municipal Education Commission—its school board—which created and implemented a set of coherent policies and practices, all aimed at ensuring that all students learn what they need to learn to be successful. The planning process Shanghai used is key, both to the quality of the plan and to its implementation.

Some might object to this example. China, after all, is a communist country; surely in that system a handful of people at the top make the plan and then order everyone else to implement it, top down, in the style of the now-defunct Soviet Union. But Shanghai's planning process turns out to be much more complicated, much more interesting, and certainly much more effective than that.

The planning process the commission now uses was developed by Minxuan Zhang. Almost 20 years ago, Zhang was the deputy director of the Shanghai Municipal Education Commission, in charge of planning. His task was to produce the five-year plan to begin in 2000. He wanted a process that would cast a wide net, be owned by a large number of stakeholders, and yet be coherent and powerful. He wanted a plan that would be visionary but actionable. He wanted the problems to be addressed and the strategies chosen to deal with them to be based on solid evidence. And he wanted a plan that would be owned so widely that everyone involved would want to implement it.

When, in 1998, Zhang started the planning process, he was determined to have a comprehensive plan that encompassed all facets of the system. He made a map of the parts and pieces of the whole system and then divided the content into 30 different areas. He then asked a Shanghai educational research institute funded by the Shanghai Municipal Education Commission to conduct a program of research on each of those areas, to gather the relevant facts, analyze the challenges, and present the relevant research. The research institute wrote a solicitation for research proposals and selected the best ones received. They selected 45 teams to cover the 30 components of the plan.

To make sure that this strategy would result in a coherent plan, Zhang had shared with all the participants a set of "themes" he had in mind for the plan that were intended to provide a unifying framework for it, something like the analysis with which we began this chapter. Thus the question for the participants in this first phase was not what the literature said in the abstract, but what it said about what would be required to address the context described by the themes.

Zhang asked the mayor to provide funds that would enable many key officials, other stakeholders, and groups to hold meetings to discuss the education challenges in Shanghai and to provide advice to the commission. The results of the research were made available to these groups.

Then Zhang asked three teams to each take the next step in the process. The three teams, working independently, were to take all the research that had been done and all the advice that had come from all the meetings and put together a draft plan. The teams were located at East China Normal University, the Shanghai Academy of Social Sciences, and the Shanghai Institute of Education Sciences.

When the three draft plans were finished, Zhang asked the heads of the three teams to present their ideas and plans at a meeting that included the mayor, the vice mayors, the heads of various key commissions, and other senior Shanghai officials. That group engaged in a lively discussion of the issues and the proposals for dealing with them.

Then Zhang called the three teams together. He told them he needed only one plan. He would give them two weeks to produce it.

When the merged plan had been produced, Zhang shared it with the central government in Beijing, education commissions in nearby provinces, UNESCO, the Hong Kong education authorities, and others. The draft was revised numerous times on the basis of several rounds of feedback and sent again to the national government in Beijing for final approval, after which the plan was adopted.

Was this bottom-up planning or top-down planning? The answer is that it is a brilliant combination of both. At no point did Zhang, the member of the commission in charge of planning, sit down and write the plan. He got other people to do that and, in the process, produced a long list of people in and out of government who owned the plan. Although many were involved, and many ended up owning the plan that was produced, the plan was still coherent and powerful.

The various parts of the Shanghai education system had been consulted throughout the process and the views of professional educators taken into account. They had been asked in the final stages of preparation to present plans for implementing the proposals being made. So the broader plan included a detailed implementation plan. Each bureau in the commission itself had a plan, and each school district had an implementation plan. When the broader plan was approved, the system was ready to go. Everyone knew what he or she needed to do.

This plan had a strong theme, a driving idea, which gave it that coherence. Because Zhang turned to two teams outside his bureaucracy to take key roles in producing the plan, it was written from a fresh and wider perspective than it would have been had the school system itself written it. But, because one of the three teams came from close to the system and the people who would have to implement it were deeply involved in producing the implementation plans, they were not standing in the wings with their arms crossed in mute defiance when the plan was finally approved.

The Shanghai planning process is not an empty formality. It produces widespread and deep changes in practice at every level of the system. It is still used in Shanghai and, now, by many other Chinese education authorities (Zhang, Ding, & Xu, 2016).

Should you use a process like the one just described? Maybe. Maybe not. You may not have the kind of institutional resources Zhang had to draw on. Your school board may not have as much power to engage those resources as Zhang's board did. You might want to follow a similar process but do it in a very different way. Or you might need a very different process altogether. We did not share this planning process with you because we think you should copy it, but because we thought it might stimulate you to think about planning in a different way and to come up with your own process using similar principles but different strategies.

Other Planning Models to Consider

Some other examples of the sort of planning we have in mind might be useful.

In 1997, when Great Britain handed Hong Kong back to the Chinese, the new government initiated a process intended to come up with a new plan for Hong Kong education that reflected the enormous changes taking place in the Hong Kong economy. Years earlier, Hong Kong was a trading city that was also home to low-skill, low-price manufacturing firms selling all over the world. But, when Deng Xiaoping opened up the mainland, in 1979, that began changing. Foreign investment firms went to Hong Kong trading firms to arrange access to mainland manufacturing capacity. Hong Kong became a global center for finance, especially for investment in Asia. Real estate prices skyrocketed, to the point that low-value-added firms could no longer afford to locate there. High-value-added manufacturing and services grew rapidly. High-powered consulting firms opened offices in Hong Kong, as did multinationals of all sorts. The skills that had been more than sufficient for working on the factory floors of firms making low-tech, low-value-added products were no longer sufficient. Hong Kong had to completely rethink its education and training needs to accommodate a swift decline in the need for low-skilled workers and a complementary new need for legions of high-skilled workers.

Fanny Law, the dynamic education secretary in the new government; Anthony Leung, a prominent business leader; and Kai Ming Cheng, then the provost at Hong Kong University, led the Hong Kong community in a two-year process to build the new education plan. Cheng had done extensive research on the evolving needs of the business community, which were shared widely with many stakeholder groups. The leaders met with thousands of people in hundreds of groups, transcribing the meetings and carefully analyzing what people from all walks of life had said. The plan went through multiple iterations in response to comments on the draft. When the planners were done, there was broad and deep support for a plan that represented a sharp departure from the previous policies and practices and laid the base for an ambitious program of broad education reform that has served Hong Kong well. Few Americans would put up with a planning process that took this long. But it is not unusual for Asian governments to take much longer than Americans to deliberately engage broad communities in planning important undertakings. Their view is that an investment of this sort reaps handsome dividends later in much broader and deeper support for changes that are often more sweeping than could be undertaken without this approach to planning. They would argue that taking more time up front to involve all the relevant stakeholders saves a lot of time later and results in more complete implementation.[2]

Singapore presents another approach to planning that is worth considering. Several things distinguish Singapore's planning style. The first is the close connection among planning for the economy, planning for education, and planning for job training. The second is the close coordination among all the relevant parts of government. The third is the attention given to planning for implementation.

Ever since Singapore left the Malaysian Federation and became independent in 1965, its government has been focused on economic growth. Its Economic Development Board was made responsible from the outset for recruiting foreign-invested firms to Singapore to fuel that growth. In the first stage, right after independence, its goal was to attract foreign firms interested in taking advantage of Singapore's low-cost labor and inexpensive facilities. At that stage the government focused its attention on the skills side on increasing adult literacy; educating and training teachers to offer public education at the primary level;

---

2. This description of planning in Hong Kong for major changes in their education system under the new Hong Kong government is based on multiple interviews conducted by NCEE with Professor Kai Ming Cheng of Hong Kong University.

and training enough carpenters, masons, and electricians to build the relatively simple structures needed to attract foreign-invested firms. All the attention was on the basics in academics and vocational education.

But then, in one carefully sequenced move after another, the Economic Development Board of Singapore raised its sights, first from low-skill, low-value-added manufacturing to high-value-added manufacturing foreign-invested firms; then to high-tech global manufacturing firms; then to attracting global financial services, telecommunications, oil industry and aircraft service firms; and then to building their own indigenous firms at a world-class level in these and other areas. At each of these stages, as they moved up the global economic ladder, the government laid a plan to develop a workforce with the education and skills needed to ascend to the next step in their economic development plan. In the United States, we tend to ask the businesses that are already there in our city or state what they think their skill needs will be over the period to be planned for. The Singaporeans asked themselves what sort of businesses they wanted to have and then built the workforce that would be needed to attract and support those businesses.

They did this with close coordination among the Economic Development Board, the Ministry of Manpower, the Ministry of Education, and other agencies. It helped a lot that Singapore rotates its key ministers and executives among its agencies, so their primary loyalty is to what is good for Singapore, not what is good for their agency or their department within their agency.

Many observers have commented on the attention that Singapore gives to planning for implementation. Recall that in the Shanghai planning system, the implementation plan is part of the plan itself, not a supplement to it. The same is true in Singapore, where as much time and attention are given to implementation planning as to the development of the plan itself. Each stage of implementation is laid out in detail and responsibilities are assigned in the plan. Nothing is left to chance, and executives are held responsible for carrying out their assignments. Bonuses and promotions depend on their success. The result is that the implementation plan is not there just to get the funds but is regarded as an operational road map to which the parties are actually committed (Tucker, 2012).

No set of stories about planning for education reform at the scale of a whole state system would be complete without the story of Massachusetts. It is no accident that Massachusetts is way ahead of any other state on the National Assessment of Educational Progress league tables and compares well to the top performers outside the United States. Of all the U.S. states, Massachusetts has done the best job of implementing the kinds of policies and practices described by the nine building blocks, not selecting a set of silver bullets but rather creating an effective system as we define that term.

The Massachusetts Miracle

In 2005, Massachusetts leaped to the head of all the states in performance on the National Assessment of Educational Progress, and it has remained the nation's highest-performing state ever since. To many in the state, that success is the fruit of legislation passed more than a decade earlier.

The legislation, known as the Education Reform Act of 1993, was the result of a broad consensus that included Republican Governor William Weld, the Democratic legislature, teachers' unions, the business community, and education reformers. But one individual played a key role: Jack Rennie. Rennie, the CEO of Pacer Systems Inc., a leading information technology company, had five children and was a volunteer in schools, and he took an active interest in education policy. He founded an organization called the Massachusetts Business Alliance for Education, which studied reform efforts around the country. The group was particularly impressed with the Kentucky Education Reform Act, which completely overhauled the education system in that state, creating a systemic approach centered around standards for student performance. The Business Alliance produced a report, titled *Every Child a Winner*, that called for a similar systemic approach in the Bay State.

Passing the law required what Rennie called a "grand bargain." As David Driscoll, who was then the deputy commissioner of education and later commissioner, explained, the bargain went like this: "We will give you the tools, but we will hold you accountable." Both parts were necessary, Driscoll said. The accountability was necessary to create the incentives for schools to improve. But, he said, "we can't expect you to change without the tools."

Specifically, the law created a new statewide testing system with a test set to high standards that students would have to pass to graduate from high school; created a new teacher-licensure test and a requirement that teachers would have to complete professional development every five years to maintain their licenses; ended tenure for principals and gave them the authority to hire teachers; authorized charter schools; and set higher standards for school and district accountability. The tools came in the form of a major increase in funding: an additional $2 billion over seven years.

The Massachusetts reforms, unlike those of any other state, reflected in their scope and character the key features of the education systems of the top-performing countries. But what is also unique is that the state stuck with it for more than two decades. Despite changes in leadership, through both Republican and Democratic administrations, the key provisions of the law have remained intact. Even so, state officials met resistance. Driscoll recalled that there were numerous protests against the graduation-test requirement and numerous attempts to scuttle it. Critics charged that it would be very unfair to low-income and minority students, who would not be able to pass it. But the state officials held fast. "[Acting Governor Jane] Swift used to say, 'Anybody waiting for Driscoll and me to blink, I'm not blinking.'"

The results silenced critics. The first time the graduation test counted, in 2001, 68 percent of 10th graders passed the mathematics portion and 72 percent passed the English portion. But students had multiple opportunities to pass the test before graduation, and ultimately, 95 percent of the class of 2003 passed the test. "We set the standards high," Driscoll said. "But they were achievable."

Driscoll and the other state leaders were betting that almost all the students could perform at much higher levels if the expectations for their performance were raised and they got the support they needed to do it. They won that bet. Other states, at about the same time, bet that they would get to high standards if they started with much lower standards and ratcheted them up slowly. Those states are still far behind Massachusetts.

The Massachusetts Education Reform Act was passed in 1993. The building of a broad coalition of stakeholders and the development of a grand political bargain that became the lever for creating a truly systemic solution stable enough to weather decades of political changes stand as mute testimony to a durable planning process that produced results as impressive as those produced in Shanghai. Since the Massachusetts Education Reform Act was passed, Massachusetts has entered the ranks of the world's top performers and pulled away from all the other American states in the rankings of performance on the National Assessment of Educational Progress (U.S. Department of Education, 2015a).

In Chapter 4, we will look inside the first subsystem you will need to build so that you can see how the top performers have approached that arena. We will help you think about how you, too, might approach it.

4

Powerful, Coherent Instructional Systems—Wrapped in Credentials That Make Sense

In Chapter 2, you learned that the top performers have carefully crafted instructional systems, with clearly delineated pathways through the system that lead to important gateways. In Chapter 3, you learned about the aspirations for student performance that have shaped goals for learning in top-performing systems. In this chapter, you will see how those learning goals have shaped the content of instruction, expectations for learning experiences and standards, and the way student progress is measured. You will learn how the top performers take all of these elements—learning goals, standards for student performance, curriculum frameworks, course descriptions and syllabi, instructional materials, pedagogies, assessment, development trajectories, learning pathways and gateways, extracurricular activities, and sports—and weave them together into intricate learning systems that produce some of the world's best results.

Goals for Student Learning

We begin by considering the goals for student learning from the vision presented in Chapter 3. In some respects, the goals contained in that vision are little different from the aims for education that have been embraced by American educators for a century or more. In other respects, they are radically different.

What Hasn't Changed

Despite the technology revolution, there is almost nothing new about the goals we should set for students. What Harriet Minor saw in the Common Core is what the best teachers have always wanted for their students in the formal curriculum: deep understanding of the subjects they study. The best teachers have tried their best to develop in their students the ability to analyze, synthesize, question, reason, think for themselves, and think outside the box. They've targeted the ability to write about complex matters clearly, concisely and, when required, in a compelling way; the ability to use mathematics fluently for a wide variety of purposes; and the ability to appreciate the power of the scientific method and gain a good grasp of the big ideas in the sciences and technology that have revolutionized the modern world. They have always known that we study history not to accumulate a storage bin of events and dates and battles and changes of government but to understand the forces behind those events and the way humans have reacted to those forces over time, so that students can approach their duties as citizens with an understanding of the importance of the institutions of freedom and democracy.

What we have recently been taught to think of as 21st century skills—things like the ability to solve complex problems creatively and effectively, to lead others but also to contribute effectively as a team member, to work independently but also collaboratively, to plan a complex project and manage it to completion on time, and to use modern information technology effectively—are not 21st century skills at all.

The Duke of Wellington is claimed to have said, nearly two centuries ago, that England's victory against Napoleon at Waterloo was won on the playing fields of Eton. The idea that participation in sports prepares students for both teamwork and leadership is hardly new, no more so than the idea that participation in student government prepares students to be good citizens.

The best educators have always cared deeply about more than all that. The best teachers have seen themselves not just teaching subjects in the curriculum or even just helping students to learn what is expected of them as workers. They have always cared very much about the kind of people their charges would grow up to be—not just smart and competent, but also courageous, empathetic, tolerant, caring, compassionate, hard-working, decent, generous, indefatigable, and confident in the pursuit of their aims—good people who would want to do the right thing when no one was looking. They have always hoped to kindle in their students a love of learning that continues through life.

What's Stunningly New

Given what we said in Chapter 3 about the direction being taken by advanced intelligent technologies, you might reasonably ask why we wasted your time with all that only to say that the aims of educators in the future ought to be pretty much what they were in the past. Here is what is radically different about these aims.

Although good teachers in all kinds of American schools have long embraced these aims, the system did not. The mass education system we have now, the outlines of which emerged early in the 20th century, had much more modest aims for students. The goals just described were the goals for only the elite, a tiny fraction of the population. What is revolutionary about the goals we just described is that it is now absolutely necessary for all children to be as well educated as the very privileged children were. Why? Because the jobs for those who up until now needed only modest skills are disappearing quickly. The kinds of jobs that will enable people to earn a decent living will require a much higher level of skills and very different kinds of skills than those that previously sustained most people. This is a huge departure from everything that has gone before, because a large percentage of our children, whose education in the current system does not do enough to help them foster these skills, will be unemployable or working for miserable wages in the economy that appears to lie ahead. It is not possible to educate virtually all students to an elite standard with the system we have, so we need a new instructional system.

Why We Have to Abandon the Sorting System

Why can't we accomplish our new goals by tweaking the system we have? Why can't we just identify the best instructional practices in our current system and apply them everywhere? If they work for some students, why wouldn't they work for all?

They won't work because the American education system operates as a giant sorting system, and a sorting system cannot be used to produce the results the nation now needs. Suppose you are a farmer in the egg business. You get eggs from lots of farms. Some are extra large, some large, some medium, and some small. You go to an agricultural machinery company and purchase an egg-sorting machine. You put all the eggs in one end and out the other come egg cartons, with only one size of eggs in each carton. You would never think your egg-sorting machine would turn out cartons that contained nothing but extra large eggs if you were feeding eggs of many sizes into it.

In the mass-production age, we did not need many professionals and managers. We did not need many craftsmen, either. We had the selective college track for the former and an often selective vocational track for the latter. Everyone else went into the general track. That was at the end, in high school. But the sorting did not begin in high school. It began in 1st grade with the robins and the bluebirds. In overwhelming numbers, the kids from the wrong side of the tracks went in with the other robins and the ones from the right side of the tracks went into the bluebirds. There was nothing mean about this. American teachers were taught by American psychologists that some kids had the genes for academics and others simply did not. Not expecting very much from low-income, minority kids was a matter of not expecting more than they could possibly do.

This sorting within the school was combined with the sorting among school districts. Basing school finance on local property wealth meant that, over time, wealthy students went to school with other wealthy students and poor students went to school with other poor students. The wealthiest students got the best of everything, the poor ones the worst. This proved to be a very efficient system. In this way, the United States concentrated its best resources for education—its best teachers, schools, and everything else—on the students who were easiest to educate to very high levels. If the best teachers, the best physical facilities, and the best of everything else had been distributed more evenly, it would have been much more difficult and expensive to produce the small number of absolutely first-rate scientists, engineers, executives, doctors, attorneys, generals, and political leaders that have made the United States the sole remaining superpower.

This system had consequences. Because students were sorted into ability groups from their first year in school and expectations for each group were different, the students who started out behind got further and further behind. Students who were called gifted and for whom expectations were high were pushed ahead. Students who were sorted into classes and schools where expectations were very low wound up in social groups in which students who performed well were ostracized. Students sorted into classes and schools where expectations were high were ostracized if they performed badly. The most experienced and best teachers wanted to work in districts and schools serving students in the upper tracks, with students who were eager to learn and easy to control, and the most inexperienced and least effective teachers were stuck with those who were the hardest to discipline and the most challenging to get interested in learning something. Along the trajectory of a student's experience in school, as the tracks hardened, the students who started out in the lowest tracks fell further behind until, by the time they got to high school, they were often years behind. Many were desperately faking the ability to read anything at all and, deeply ashamed and angry, they could not wait to drop out of school.

Though the United States has dropped many of the formalisms of tracking, the essence remains alive and well. If the aim is to get everyone to a high standard, then the standard must be high and constant, and the time taken to reach it variable, which is the exact opposite of the system we now have, in which the time is held constant and the standard achieved varies with the student. We cannot sort our way to greatness.

How Would a New System Work?

We can see the outlines of a new system in the countries that have constructed much higher performing systems. One part of the system, the part that we will deal with in this chapter, has to do with the standards for student achievement, and the way those standards are translated into curriculum, course syllabi, instructional materials, teaching methods, and student assessment. No less important is the way students are expected to progress through the curriculum, how many are expected to achieve how much at what rate of progress, the strategies used to keep all students on track, and the way the system provides for student choice and variety while making sure that all students master a Common Core curriculum that will serve as a sturdy foundation of learning for the rest of their lives, no matter what path they take.

To show you how the top performers accomplish these goals, we provide here an overview of the strategies they use. Not all of these countries do all of these things. To show you how these strategies fit together in one seamless system, we will illustrate the overall design with examples, mostly from Singapore.

A System of Pathways and Gateways

The top performers see their education systems as a pattern of pathways and gateways for students. The pathways through the system are clear and populated with challenging curriculum that is fully supported. Some lead to jobs right out of what we think of as high school; all of them lead to further education. The pathways are punctuated by gateways that are set to high standards. At each gateway there are choices to be made. The number of gateways varies from country to country, but the typical pattern is to have a major gateway at the end of what we think of as the 10th grade, or age 16, and another two or three years later, at the end of high school. To get through each gate, a student has to demonstrate a specified level of knowledge and skills, by getting high grades in designated coursework, passing a test, or both. The pathways available on the other side of the gate depend on the courses taken and the grades achieved. For each of the possible pathways, the courses are mostly required and are laid out in a sequence. The exams taken at the gateways are external exams, so that no one can get a better grade by twisting anyone's arm. In most of these countries, the first stretch, from the first day of compulsory school to the end of what we think of as grade 10, is when the students are expected to master the Common Core curriculum. This curriculum is the foundation for everything that comes later. It is set to internationally benchmarked standards and includes the official language of schooling, mathematics, the sciences, and much more.

Though the idea of a demanding Common Core curriculum is important, in practice the curriculum is not necessarily identical for all students. We'll use Singapore to illustrate the point. You can think about their curriculum as including several different tracks. One is what you might think of as the standard academic track. Another is a souped-up version of the standard academic track, with more challenging work for students deemed to be high performing. The bottom track lacks some of the topics in the standard track but would nonetheless be regarded as a tough curriculum in most school districts in the United States. Then there is another track that is also regarded as a standard track, but it is heavily oriented toward applied work. Again, Americans would likely regard the academics quite demanding in this track. Most of the students in this bottom track are headed toward a vocational education program in their last two years of high school.

You will be aghast. Just a moment ago, we were decrying the evils of tracking. Now, here we are, embracing a tracking system. But there is a difference, and the difference is very important. In this case, the whole system is set up so that all but the most severely handicapped students are expected to meet a high, internationally benchmarked standard of academic achievement, including students who choose the vocational path. That means that the *least* accomplished of them graduate knowing more and being able to do more than the average American high school graduate. The tracking system is set up to make sure that almost all students reach that standard. It is not set up to evade that standard. The whole point of the tracking system is to make sure that the least accomplished students have the time and support they need to reach the standard, no matter what it takes. That is a very different type of tracking system than the kind commonly found in the United States.

When we visit middle and high schools in the top-performing countries, their principals tell us that they do not have to worry about students who enter their schools from their feeder schools being years behind where they should be. The reason that the students in their bottom quartile do so well is that they have not been falling further and further behind their classmates as they have gone through the system.

Again, we will put the spotlight on Singapore to illustrate the point. The curriculum that the lowest quartile of students is taking is demanding but lean. There are no frills. The curriculum that the top quartile of students is taking is the same curriculum but is enriched, with additional topics and deeper work in the core.

For the students at the very bottom of the distribution, the time allotted to the core is extended, all the way to the end of high school, if necessary. "No Child Left Behind" was a slogan in the United States, but it is a reality in Singapore. The whole system is geared toward making sure that almost every student achieves that standard. Not only do students who need more time get it, with more years to reach the standard at the end, but they come in on Saturdays, have extended days, or even work with their teachers into the evening. All through the grades, teachers are expected to closely monitor their students' progress, not just quarter by quarter, but day by day and minute by minute, and to add time and other resources if they start to fall behind. Students are not accumulating credits. Their actual performance is being monitored against a clearly defined common curriculum using the same external measures used throughout the country.

When the students have mastered the common curriculum, usually in 10 years, they go their own way, depending in part on what they want to do and in part on how well they have done up to that point. This sounds like a more rigid system than it actually is. In Singapore, parents can request that their children be assigned to a higher track than their performance to date would entitle them to and that preference is honored. But if the student cannot keep up, then he or she is reassigned to the original placement. At the 10th grade gateway, it is again possible to move across pathways if the student is willing to take additional coursework and makes the required grades. In this way, students can move from vocational education and training pathways to academic ones and vice versa, or students can choose to do both, if they want the career insurance such a choice might provide.

There are no dead ends in this system. Students in Singapore who are in the standard academic program in high school can go on to a polytechnic and, if they want to and take the right courses, can go from there into university and graduate school. Or they can go into a junior college and straight to university. Students who are in the high school-level vocational program can go right into the job market or go on to polytechnic and then university and graduate school if they want to, if they take the right courses and get the right grades. In this system, the bottom quartile performs above the average American student and the top quartile leaves high school two to three years ahead of the average American student.

The Singaporeans are not 10 feet tall, any more than the Japanese engineers who were beating Xerox were 10 feet tall. How do they do it? The first part of the answer is the system of pathways and gateways just described. But that is not all there is to it. There is also the question of what these countries do to ensure that their students can get these qualifications. That requires a carefully designed instructional system consisting of tightly aligned standards, curriculum frameworks, course syllabi, instructional materials, and assessments. We turn now to a description of a typical instructional system in a top-performing country.

Quality Standards, and the Curricula and Syllabi Based on Them

When we say "academic standards" in the United States, what comes to mind are the Common Core State Standards for English language arts and mathematics and the Next Generation Science Standards. You will find something very similar in the top-performing countries, but not just for their native language, mathematics, and the sciences. The standards typically cover, in addition, foreign languages, technology, national history, world history, geography, music, and the arts.

In the United States, academic standards are usually thought of as narrative statements about what students should know and be able to do. But in the typical top-performing country, there is more. The standards also include examples of student work that meets the standard (that is, gets a good grade) and a clear, detailed statement identifying the specific features of the student work that justified that grade. The examples of student work are usually drawn from actual student work done in response to the prompts in the national examinations, which typically require long-form essays in response. This is especially important for low-income and minority students, who may have less access to examples of good writing, good mathematical reasoning, or good historical analysis than students from more favored backgrounds.

An example of this type of performance standard comes from New Zealand. That country's national curriculum specifies the achievement levels that indicate a progression of learning from year 1 to year 13, along with samples of student work that exemplify the standards—and annotations to point out the qualities of the work that demonstrate the standards.

Year 4 Writing Standard, New Zealand National Curriculum

By the end of year 4, students are required to create a variety of texts in order to think about, record, and communicate experiences, ideas, and information across the curriculum. To meet the standard, students draw on the knowledge, skills, and attitudes for writing described in the *Literacy Learning Progressions* for students at this level.

As part of their learning in English, the students in this year 4 class are writing to form and express ideas based on a significant personal experience. Each student is writing a recount of a scary experience that they think will interest and engage their audience.

This example illustrates aspects of the task and text and demonstrates how a student engages with both task and text to meet the writing demands of the curriculum. A number of such examples would be used to inform the overall teacher judgment for this student.

> "Maraea, please go feed your rabbit!" Mum called from the hallway. "Okay," I said back and got a bucket to put some grass in for Aorha (my rabbit). So there I was getting some grass for Aorha and as I was about to leave I saw a ram. It was approching me. I saw it stare at me a scary look like it was going to hurt me. I droped the buket and ran. I glanced back and it was chasing me. I was so close to the fence so I started climbing it. The ram caught my pants when I was almost over. I screamed as I pulled it to the ground. But it finally let go so I jumped up, gbabed the buket, chuked it over the fence then I climbed over the fence before the ram could get me. I lay on the grass relieved that I was safe. I looked in the buket nothing. "Oh well" I said "she'll just have to put up with no grass tonight". As I walked back home I glanced back. I saw the ram. It was staring at me. I quickly turned away. I was safe.

Annotations:

- The student opens the recount with direct speech to engage the reader's interest in the situation from the beginning.
- In her recount, the student records the main actions, thoughts, and feelings clearly and in sequence, using a variety of simple connectives ("as," "so," "when")
- She supports the main points of her recount with simple detail to give the reader a clear and engaging picture of the situation (particularly the actions the narrator takes as the ram chases and grabs her). The student uses precise verbs for greater clarity (e.g., "approching," "stare," "glanced"). She is familiar with some spelling patterns ("stare," "scary") but needs to develop a stronger knowledge of other common patterns ("approching," "droped," "buket").
- The student uses a variety of sentence structures and achieves some excitement and movement in the text by varying the sentence lengths. She uses speech and inner reflections to help give the recount a personal voice.

Quality standards, and the curricula and syllabi based on them, give students a visceral feel for the kind of work required for success. The top performers typically use the standards to develop curriculum frameworks that spell out in detail the progression of topics to be studied, in sequence in each subject as the student goes through the grades, sometimes by grade, sometimes by grade span. The curriculum frameworks reflect both the logic of the subject and the normal developmental trajectory of students who study those subjects. Development of the curriculum frameworks begins with the specification of what the student is supposed to know and be able to do to get the first qualification, usually at the end of 10th grade, and then backs down to the 1st grade, making sure that, at each grade level or grade span, the student gets what is needed to master the next topic or stage of development in the curriculum. Nothing extraneous is included, and nothing essential is left out. The developers make sure there is enough time for all students to master each topic before moving on, so that no one will be left behind. As we said earlier, some students may need more time and assistance outside the regular classroom hours allotted to the topic, and that extra time and assistance is provided along the way, so that all students can keep up in class.

In many countries, this curriculum framework is then used to create course syllabi for each course in the sequence. The syllabi do what any good syllabus does: describe what is supposed to be learned in the course; the topics to be covered; the books and other materials the student is expected to read; the papers, projects, or other products the student is expected to produce; and the way the student will be assessed. In many cases they also indicate how much each exam, project, or product will count in the final grade (see the example from New South Wales, Australia).

Syllabus for History, New South Wales, Australia

The Australian curriculum is being implemented in New South Wales through new syllabi developed by BOSTES for English, Mathematics, Science and Technology, History, and Geography.

The new K–10 syllabi include agreed-upon Australian curriculum content and content that clarifies learning in kindergarten to year 10. The stage statements for Early Stage 1 to Stage 5 reflect the intent of the Australian curriculum achievement standards.

The syllabi identify the knowledge, understanding, skills, values, and attitudes that students are expected to develop at each stage, from kindergarten to year 10.

Teachers will continue to have flexibility to make decisions about the sequence of learning; the emphasis to be given to particular areas of content; and any adjustments required based on the needs, interests, and abilities of their students.

The syllabi have been designed to be taught within the BOSTES recommended percentages for each key learning area in a typical school week.

Assessment for learning continues to be an essential component of the K–10 syllabi.

Early Stage 1–Stage 3

Early Stage 1	**Stage 1**
Personal and Family Histories	Present and Past Family Life The Past in the Present
Stage 2	**Stage 3**
Community and Remembrance First Contacts	The Australian Colonies Australia as a Nation

Stage 4

The Ancient World [50 hours minimum teaching time]

Overview
The overview is approximately 10 percent of teaching time of *The Ancient World*. The content from the overview may be used as an overall introduction to, or may be integrated with, Depth Studies 1–3.

Depth Study 1	**Depth Study 2**	**Depth Study 3**
Investigating the Ancient Past (including ancient Australia)	*The Mediterranean World* ONE of the following to be studied: Egypt *Or* Greece *Or* Rome	*The Asian World* ONE of the following to be studied: India *Or* China

Syllabus for History, New South Wales, Australia *(continued)*

The Ancient to the Modern World [50 hours minimum teaching time]

Overview

The overview is approximately 10 percent of teaching time of *The Ancient to the Modern World*. The content from the overview may be used as an overall introduction to, or may be integrated with, Depth Studies 4–6.

Depth Study 4	Depth Study 5	Depth Study 6
The Western and Islamic World ONE of the following to be studied: The Vikings *Or* Medieval Europe *Or* The Ottoman Empire *Or* Renaissance Italy	*The Asia-Pacific World* ONE of the following to be studied: Angkor/Khmer Empire *Or* Japan Under the Shoguns *Or* The Polynesian Expansion Across the Pacific	*Expanding Contacts* ONE of the following to be studied: Mongol Expansion *Or* The Black Death in Asia, Europe, and Africa *Or* The Spanish Conquest of the Americas *Or* Aboriginal and Indigenous Peoples, Colonisation, and Contact History

All students must complete a site study in Stage 4. A virtual site study can be used if appropriate.

Stage 5

The Making of the Modern World [50 hours minimum teaching time]

For Stage 5, the two overviews and four of the six depth studies must be studied. Depth Studies 3 and 4, core studies, are to be studied by all students.

Overview

The overview is approximately 10 percent of teaching time of *The Making of the Modern World*. The content from the overview may be used as an overall introduction to, or may be integrated with, Depth Studies 1–3.

Depth Study 1	**Depth Study 2**	**Core Study–Depth Study 3**
Making a Better World?	*Australia and Asia*	*Australians at War*
ONE of the following to be studied:	ONE of the following to be studied:	*(World Wars I and II)*
The Industrial Revolution	Making a Nation	**Mandatory study**
Or	*Or*	
Movement of Peoples	Asia and the World	
Or		
Progressive Ideas and Movements		

Syllabus for History, New South Wales, Australia *(continued)*

The Modern World and Australia [50 hours minimum teaching time]

Overview

The overview is approximately 10 percent of teaching time of *The Modern World and Australia*. The content from the overview may be used as an overall introduction to, or may be integrated with, Depth Studies 4–6.

Core Study–Depth Study 4	Depth Study 5	Depth Study 6
Rights and Freedoms (1945–present)	*The Globalising World*	*School-developed topic drawn from either of the overviews, such as*
Mandatory study	ONE of the following to be studied:	Australia in the Vietnam War Era
	Popular culture	*Or*
	Or	The Holocaust
	The environment movement	*Or*
	Or	Women's History
	Migration experiences	*Or*
		UN Peacekeeping
		Or
		A Decade Study
		Or
		The Gulf Wars and the War in Afghanistan
		A list of suggested topics is provided in **Depth Study 6** in Stage 6

All students must complete a site study (a virtual site study may be used, if appropriate) in Stage 5.

As you can see from this example, the syllabi in top-performing countries do not dictate that every student will be on the same page of the same textbook every day. That stereotype has led many in the United States to fear a "national curriculum." In fact, U.S. states, such as Massachusetts, the nation's top performer, have developed curriculum frameworks that provide important guidance to teachers. The syllabi go a step forward, but they do not constrain teachers.

The syllabi do not include lesson plans. Indeed, teachers have broad latitude, as you will see in Chapter 6, to design lesson plans that fit their students and their personal preferences. The structure provided by the aligned standards, curriculum framework, syllabi, and instructional materials makes it much more likely than in the United States that all students—rich and poor, majority and minority—will get the same rich curriculum, be held to the same high standards, and have access to a strong system of support to enable them to reach the standards.

In many of the top-performing countries, these demanding courses have an enriched version, and teachers are even free to deviate from the course designs if their students are making good progress toward the standards. The supports we have just described are there for everyone who needs them.

Further, because the curriculum framework is the same everywhere, students who move from school to school can pick up where they left off. Teachers in grade 6 can count on students coming in from grade 5 to be ready for the lesson plans they have designed, without missing a beat. Schools of education know what teachers at each grade level and subject have to know and be able to teach. All these parts and pieces work together to provide a strong web of support to all kinds of students as they go through a very demanding program.

Assessment in the Top-Performing Countries

In top-performing countries, the state creates not only the course syllabi but also the examinations, which are based on the course design as captured in the syllabus. They are end-of-course examinations, not tests of the usual American sort that are designed to be curriculum neutral. The big exception in some countries, and a major bone of contention, is the university entrance examinations, which are viewed widely as an impediment to the achievement of national goals in elementary and secondary education.

Though these exams may contain some multiple-choice questions, they typically rely mainly on essay-type questions and responses. It would be much cheaper to use multiple-choice, computer-scored examinations, but these countries have chosen to use mainly essay-based, human-scored examinations because they want to measure a much wider range of complex skills than they think multiple-choice exams can accurately measure. The state is responsible for issuing the exams and scoring them. The scoring is usually done by teachers, under the supervision of a testing authority that sees to it that professional standards of reliability and validity are met in exam construction and scoring. Scoring these exams is usually viewed as part of the teacher's job, and teachers find that the experience is strong professional learning because they develop a better understanding of what kind of work students need to do to succeed.

The results of these exams provide the exemplars of student work we mentioned earlier. They are typically posted on the ministry website after the exams are given, often along with commentary from the examination authority explaining why the responses got good grades.

When American students take a test, their feedback is a score related to the number of test items answered correctly and, sometimes, information about how their score compared to the scores of other students taking the test. That tells the students nothing about what they did well and what they need to work on. It gives no feeling at all about the target they should be aiming for. It is a game of blind man's bluff.

That might not have mattered when the aim of schooling was to make sure the student could add a column of figures and get the right answer or to make sure that the student could produce a sentence with subject and object in the right places. But it matters greatly when the student has to figure out how to frame a real-world situation in mathematical terms and then proceed to solve the problem so framed in a series of separate mathematical operations. Or when the student is called on to provide a written analysis of the options facing a policymaker and argue persuasively for one of them.

The big gateway tests we have described are often the only tests required by the state in a student's whole career in school. In Finland, the only exam required for all students is the college entrance examination; Finland tests students on a sample basis in grades 6 and 9. In many countries, the only required test is at the end of the common curriculum, usually the end of 10th grade and at the end of whatever comes next, which is usually a university preparation program culminating in a university qualification or a vocational education and training program culminating in an industry-recognized qualification, a qualification for further education, or both. In some countries, there is an additional state test at the end of middle school, which is used as an entrance examination for selective high schools.

But all along the way, from 1st grade on, teachers are expected to assess their students and report the results to education officials and parents, using a combination of formative evaluation and summative evaluation of the student's progress toward the qualifications.

Building on the State Standards to Create a Top-Performing System

Most states in the United States have adopted the Common Core State Standards or standards very like them. Some have also adopted the Next Generation Science Standards. None that we know of have used these standards to develop the full panoply of curriculum and instructional supports described in this chapter. But there is no reason you cannot do this in your district, alone or in league with other likeminded districts. When you do this, keep in mind the importance of (1) setting a high minimum performance standard for all but the most severely handicapped students and (2) developing the full web of support needed to get all your students there.

Remember, too, that in the top-performing countries, the core curriculum covers not just their native language, mathematics, and science. It also typically includes technology, history, art, and music, at a minimum, and often much more, including, in Finland, philosophy. The whole system of curriculum frameworks, course syllabi, and course-based examinations applies to these subjects as well. You do not have to do this all at once, but the faster you move in this direction, the stronger your student performance will be.

College and Career Readiness Standards

Many states now have what they think of as college-and-career-ready standards or are working toward them. But these standards are often expressed in terms of a maze of scores on the SAT or ACT, accumulated course credits, completion of career and technical education course sequences, attainment of industry-recognized certificates, scores on college placement tests, or some combination of these. A score on the ACT or SAT is just that—a score. It tells neither the student nor the teacher what the student has to do to reach the standard, provides no guidance on what kind of work will meet the standard, and points to no specific curriculum that will help the student meet the standard. Most states count as an approved career and technical education program a sequence of three—sometimes four—career and technical education courses. That is roughly one course a year. No top-performing country would recognize this as serious preparation for a career in any occupation that would support a family. And simply completing such a sequence without specifying a performance test and a passing grade is not a serious standard. College placement tests have largely been discredited as measures of college readiness. Many of those who flunk them do well in college and many who pass do not. There is every reason to believe they are poor measures of what it takes to be successful in the typical college that uses them, and many higher education institutions are abandoning their use. Many states appear to be moving toward the use of occupational credentials as a substitute for academic credentials in determining college and career readiness. But the occupational credentials they are using are often based on industry clusters that are not widely recognized by employers as embodying the knowledge and skill needed to do specific entry-level jobs leading to rewarding careers. More to the point, the substitution of such a credential for a showing that the student is leaving high school ready to succeed in the typical community college is a recipe for graduating a student who will struggle economically his or her entire life. Students who do not have the academic knowledge and skill to succeed in a typical community college are students who cannot read, write, and do mathematics well enough to succeed in the kinds of jobs that will dominate the job market in the near future. To establish school-leaving standards lower than the standards needed to succeed in a typical community college is to cement in place the idea that career and technical education is for students who are no good at academics. That idea is dead and gone in most of the top-performing countries. But we pointed out that the instructional system in the top-performing countries is about much more than their qualification system.

As we said, the United States now has standards for English language arts, mathematics, and the sciences, but lacks such standards for most of the rest of the core curriculum. There are some examples of student work that meets the standards in these areas, but nowhere near the number and variety that exist in the top-performing countries and very little in the way of commentary that explains why they meet the standards. So, overall, we don't have good standards in many subjects, and the ones we have lack the richness that the standards in the top-performing countries usually have, especially the kind of richness that vulnerable students most need. No less important, such standards are almost strictly narrative, lacking in examples of student work that meets the standards and commentary on those pieces of student work that are useful as teachers and students try to understand what the standards really call for.

The United States mostly lacks strong curriculum frameworks matched to the standards. The frameworks we have are not matched to a structure of pathways and gateways, so it is unclear, for example, what part of the Common Core math standards are supposed to be mastered by all students and which should be optional and taught in the upper division of high school. We mostly lack frameworks that are carefully matched to what the research tells us about the way students actually learn the material, nor do they structure the topics to be studied in logical order or eliminate everything that does not contribute to the outcomes that define the standards for student performance at the end of grade 10.

The United States does not have a strong set of course syllabi matched to a strong curriculum framework matched to an explicit structure of pathways and gateways and curriculum frameworks set to a common set of high standards. Some states and some districts have course syllabi, but they are of uneven quality and are rarely aligned with the other elements of high-performance instructional systems. Because the United States does not have a well-developed system of course syllabi matched to the standards, we have not been able to develop a strong system of teacher education and training matched to the courses they are supposed to teach.

In the United States, the tests are usually based on the standards rather than on the courses that students take, which makes it more likely that the student will be tested on a curriculum that was never delivered. Because the two consortia tests—the Partnership for Assessment of Readiness for College and Careers (PARCC) and the Smarter Balanced Assessment Consortium (SBAC)—are heavily weighted toward multiple-choice prompts that do not require essay-type responses, neither students nor their teachers have a clear idea about what kind of student work will earn high grades—an especially serious problem for low-income students, minority students, and special education students, because expectations are typically so much lower for those students.

Because the textbook companies have produced texts they claim are aligned with the standards, though independent researchers say that is not so for most of them, teachers do not have access to commercial materials that will support a curriculum aligned with the standards. States and not-for-profit organizations are attempting to fill the void with teacher-generated curriculum, but few teachers have the time needed to develop the kind of first-class curriculum routinely developed in the top-performing countries and very little of the material and lessons produced by teachers in the United States has been properly vetted. New

York made a good start at developing materials aligned with the Common Core, and others have been working to meet that challenge, but we have yet to see anything that can match the well-developed, highly aligned instructional systems in the top-performing countries, either for the subjects covered by the Common Core or for the other subjects in the extended core curriculum for grades 1 through 10.

Most states in the United States have pieces of the structure just described in place, but much—perhaps most—of the instructional system support structure routinely available in the top-performing countries is not available in the United States.

This description of the support provided for teachers and students by a well-developed instructional system sounds a bit mechanical and the mechanics are very important, but the spirit in which the components of the system are developed is as important as the engineering of them. The Next Generation Science Standards nicely capture the spirit driving the top performers when they speak not just of the importance of the big ideas but also of the need to identify the most important ideas that cut across the sciences, and when they call for a curriculum that focuses not just on what you know but on what you can do with what you know, not just on the results science has produced but on the spirit of inquiry and the methods that have produced that knowledge. It is the same spirit that leads in assessment to an effort to capture the quality of the performances that matter most, like writing a long essay in history that captures the key differences and similarities in two eras; creating an oil painting that expresses the essence of the scene; understanding a complex problem in the real world, figuring out how to express that problem in mathematical terms, and then setting up and executing the sequence of mathematical procedures needed to answer the original practical problem; or approaching another practical problem with the toolkit a scientist would use to understand how the world in a particular microcosm actually works by generating a hypothesis and testing the hypothesis with data.

Some of you will wonder why nothing has been said thus far about instructional technology. Surely, we can learn something important from the top performers about how digital technologies can be used to educate students to higher standards and do it in ways that will be more efficient than the 19th century methods we are still using. Well, it turns out that is not the case. The United States spends more on instructional technology per student than any other advanced industrial country. But the OECD-PISA data show no relationship between expenditure on instructional technology and student performance. Even more sobering is the finding from the PIACC data that millennials in the U.S. workforce score lower on technology-enabled problem solving than the millennials in any other country whose workforce has been surveyed by OECD. This is not to say that digital technologies cannot make a difference but only that they have not done so yet. These data would seem to show that, if your aim is to improve student performance, you should be investing your funds in first-rate teachers and high-quality instructional systems, not technology.

What a New Framework Based on Top-Performing Countries Would Look Like

In this section, we describe the system we are recommending to the states we are working with. Think about how you might adapt it to the situation you face in your state.

The Qualification System

The process begins by finding out what your graduates would need to succeed in the community college or colleges nearest you. Don't ask the colleges what that standard is. They will tell you what their aspirations are, not what it actually takes to succeed in their first-year courses. Ask them if you can look at typical first-year textbooks and analyze their reading level. Ask them which is the toughest math course that first-year students will have to take and analyze the content. Ask to see papers that students are asked to write that have been graded by the instructors and use those samples to determine the real writing standard.

Now use what you have learned to set your college-and-career-ready standard. You will be surprised at how low that standard really is, but bear in mind that the majority of high school graduates are now required to take remedial courses and the majority of those who take remedial courses never get a degree. If you can get all of your students to this standard, it will make an enormous difference to your graduates' life prospects.

Establish this new college-and-career-ready standard as the standard you want a steadily rising proportion of your students to reach by the end of 10th grade and all but the students with the most significant delays to reach by the time they leave high school.

This college-and-career-ready standard will be the first big qualification for the students in your system. Once they reach it, students can then choose among the following pathways, all of which they will be ready for: (1) a demanding internationally recognized diploma program designed to get them into the most selective colleges in the world (e.g., AP International Diploma program, the International Baccalaureate program, the Cambridge Diploma program); (2) a demanding career and technical education program leading directly to a well-paying career; or (3) a complete two-year college-level degree program culminating in an associate's degree, awarded to the student along with the high school diploma on graduation.

By using the criteria for succeeding in the first year of community college as the goal for your students to achieve by the end of 10th grade, not the 12th grade, you set up every one of your students for success, whether their aim is Harvard or Stanford, a career in computer systems management, or leaving high school with a two-year college degree at zero cost to their family, ready to go to work in a good job or finish the last two years of college.

A qualifications program structured in this way would greatly improve graduation rates, and it would increase the proportion of high school graduates prepared to succeed in the world's leading selective universities, colleges, and other open-admissions institutions. It would also result in many more high school graduates prepared for entry-level jobs leading to rewarding careers that pay well. Because this structure makes it possible to earn a two-year associate's degree by the end of high school, free of charge, it would result in enormous savings to parents, students, and the state.

Those outcomes will be products not just of the structure of the qualification system just described but also of its systematic implementation in conjunction with all the other policies and practices described in this and the following chapters.

What Happens Outside of Class

The new model learning system is not just about what happens in class. Beyond creating a first-rate qualification system and a world-class system of instruction, two other things are vital. The first is what we think of the extracurricular program. The other we might think of as the heart of the matter.

The extracurricular program. We pointed out in earlier chapters that digital technologies are likely to make what is distinctly human about our students—things that our greatest educators have always prioritized, like our values, moral commitments, social and emotional skills, creative capacity, leadership ability, ability to contribute to a team effort, and the like—more important than ever.

Most of these elements of a good education cannot be taught directly. They are best learned by example or from experience, under the guidance of a skilled and dedicated mentor. These are best learned in the choir, in the school band, on the football field, in the midnight hours putting the school newspaper together, while campaigning for election for the school government, on the stage crew, by helping senior citizens in a nursing home, or while interning in a law office or apprenticing to a master boat builder.

In most high schools, these activities are voluntary and a student need not engage in any of them. Many of them have room for only a few students, and those are the students who seem to be best qualified to succeed in them. Because many schools charge for these activities, many students cannot participate. Similarly, students who have jobs after school frequently cannot participate, nor can students who have no transportation home if they stay to do these sorts of activities.

If it is true that the qualities that are best developed by activities of this sort are at least as important as what is learned in class, if the nation's battles are more likely to be won in the nursing home and in student government than in the classroom, then educators might have to rethink what is core and what is optional. Educators might need to be explicit about the qualities that these activities are intended to develop and work together to make sure that students have sufficient opportunities to develop the qualities, ensure that all students sign up for activities that could help develop them, and then track their progress to make sure no one falls through the cracks.

In this model of education, classwork is not at the center and extracurricular activities on the periphery. Both are joined together in one learning system, the purpose of which is to create a skein of linked learning experiences for students that will enable them to acquire the values, attributes, skills, and knowledge—cognitive and noncognitive—needed to succeed. Teachers organize, develop, and provide some of those experiences directly. In other cases, they just organize, mediate, and track them. Either way, the teacher is making sure that each student gets the learning experiences needed to be successful.

Top-performing countries place a strong emphasis on building such a learning system. They do so in two ways. First, the goals of education, which drive the standards, curriculum frameworks, syllabi, and assessments, are broad and encompass values and attributes as well as cognitive skills and knowledge. For example, the Alberta, Canada, Ministry of Education in 2009 conducted a broad-ranging review of its education system, with the goal of defining what an educated Albertan who graduated in 2030 would look like. The vision that emerged was this: "To inspire and enable students to achieve success and fulfillment as engaged thinkers and ethical citizens with an entrepreneurial spirit within an inclusive education system" (Alberta Education, 2010, p. 7).

Second, top-performing countries give schools and teachers a lot of latitude to provide students with the experiences and supports they need to become good people as well as good learners. This is true even in East Asian countries, belying their (undeserved) reputations as test-taking machines. The examples that follow, from Hong Kong and Singapore, show how schools can take advantage of that flexibility.

"First the heart, then the head." Now we get to what we just called the heart of the matter. A welder can be successful on the strength of her technical skills alone. A teacher cannot. A student who thinks he is destined for failure has no interest in learning. A student whose whole experience says that no adult can be trusted will not trust her teacher. A student who lives in constant fear or constant pain is not a promising candidate for instruction in long division.

Many teachers in the United States know these things and are ready to do whatever it takes to address these issues, sometimes in circumstances that would curl the hair of their most ardent critics. But many of those teachers do what they do, not because their school leaders or districts encourage them or give them incentives to do those things, but in spite of the disincentives they face. What is interesting about many of the top-performing nations, states, and provinces we have seen, especially in Asia, is the degree to which they expect this behavior, incentivize it, and celebrate it.

In Singapore, Shanghai, and Hong Kong, we have often heard the phrase "first the heart, then the head." The phrase has particular salience in schools serving children in very poor communities, often communities with many struggling families from ethnic and racial minorities.

Ho Yu College and Primary School, Hong Kong

Located far from the city center on Lantau Island, in an area that has long been home to Hong Kong's poor, Ho Yu is concrete and functional. When the principal, Lee Suet Ying, came here about 15 years ago, she found a school controlled by street gangs, the faculty cowed, their morale broken, and the students frightened and angry at a world that seemed to have abandoned them. Almost all who made it to graduation became truck and taxi drivers; got factory jobs; or cooked, washed dishes, and served customers in the countless roadside food stalls and shops.

When she arrived a little after 8:00 a.m., Lee was standing in the schoolyard with other faculty members, greeting the students. Ho Yu is a "through-train" college and primary school, meaning that it enrolls students from grades 1 through 12. We watched the older students throwing basketballs in small groups and the younger ones racing up to Lee and the other faculty members, grinning, looking for a hug and laughing when they got it, folding themselves into Lee's skirt as they did so, her hand curling around their faces in a caress that was returned in their eyes.

The students' parents were often illiterate, their homes violent, and their future bleak. When Lee first arrived, many of the students were afraid to come to the school because of the unchecked power of gangs. Expecting little from their teachers, they would sit in class sullen and unresponsive, learning little.

Her first task, Lee said, was not to educate her students— that would come later—but to get the students to trust the faculty and staff. Her top priority was to find staff who had both the desire and the skill to reach out to the students, take a personal interest in them, and help them address the problems they faced in their daily lives. Staff took the kids on trips to places they had never been before, took an interest in their personal lives, appeared in court for them when they got in trouble with the law, and helped them get a job when they could. They were there for these young people day and night, and in the process earned their trust.

It was a very slow process. It took, Lee said, five years. Which is to say that Lee paid little attention to academic achievement for five years after becoming principal of this school. She knew that she would not be able to lift the academic performance of her flock until the school had become a refuge from a very difficult world and the faculty had become people with whom the students could feel safe and, indeed, loved. The students would not have confidence in themselves and believe they had a future worth investing in until they had adults in their lives who believed in them.

To this day, the faculty is there for the students, whatever it takes. The gates open at 8:00 a.m. Classes end at 4:30 p.m. and that's when the sports and extracurricular programs begin. Most students and teachers are gone by 6:00 p.m. But many stay, partly because they are so deeply engaged in what they are doing. Lee recently tried to lock the doors at 8:30 p.m. Many teachers objected, saying that their students had nowhere else to do their homework and, in many cases, there was no one home and they wanted to make sure their students were safe. But the teachers, we said, must have their own families to go home to. Oh, said Lee, it is the younger teachers who do not yet have kids of their own who are objecting to closing the school at 8:30 p.m.

When the time came, Lee was all business. We asked whether her teachers specialized in math and science or language and social studies in the primary grades, as is so often the case in Asian schools. All my teachers, she said, have majored in the one or two subjects that they teach. Even the primary school-level teachers specialize. You cannot, she said, really teach a subject well, even at the primary school level, unless you have studied it hard at the graduate level. When students are having trouble, she said, the teachers must be able to make accurate guesses as to the nature of the student's misunderstandings. That requires deep understanding of the subject.

We asked Lee how she selected her staff. She turned to two other faculty members in the room. Both vice principals, they had been with her for 15 years. One had served at the Diocesan Boys' School, one of Hong Kong's most prestigious high schools, before coming to Ho Yu. We asked why she had made the change. Because, she said, these students needed me more. We asked Lee why she picked her. Because of her smile, she said. She explained that her vice principal had met all her academic standards, which were very high, standards on which she would not bend. But that was not enough. She was determined to have teachers who could earn the trust of the students. She wanted, she said, "Teachers who could bring sunshine into the lives of these students." The capacity to bring sunshine was just as important as deep knowledge of the subjects they would teach. She wanted teachers who would love their students and do whatever was necessary to help them succeed.

We took a tour of the school. The last classroom we visited was its pride and joy, a biotechnology lab. A few years earlier, a wealthy businessman and scientist had donated a sophisticated biotechnology laboratory, focused on genetic research, to a local university. He had included in his gift equipment that would enable the university to engage schoolchildren in the study of biotechnology and genetics, but, as it turned out, the university had no interest in educating the wider community. Lee, ever alert, seized the opportunity. The donor was delighted. Lee worked with him and with her teachers to develop a curriculum, materials, and training for the teachers. The students were off-the-wall engaged!

When we walked in, we found not only an impressive array of equipment but also carefully framed materials that did a wonderful job of explaining in simple language some rather complex topics in technology and biology. The whole instructional system was project-based. Lee explained that access to this kind of equipment gave the students the feeling that the sky was the limit for them if they were willing to put in the hard work needed to gain the necessary skills;

they were valued not just by the staff of the school, but by the wider community as well.

Then Lee took us outside to a paved parking space marked off by carefully painted yellow lines. Parked with perfect geometric accuracy within those lines was a bus. She explained that they had worked with the donor, who had paid for it all, to custom design every facet of that bus apart from the frame and its Volvo power train. It was gorgeous. Inside was a mobile laboratory, outfitted to enable everyone from the very young to the very old to learn about biotechnology, not just by reading about it or watching videos but by *doing* it. It was a bit like a modern crime lab, a place where the visitor could analyze DNA in a tissue sample. It was, we thought, impossible to visit this bus and not walk away excited about biotechnology, what it is, how it works, and what it could accomplish. The bus goes all over Hong Kong, a roving educational facility, realizing the donor's dream.

Today, Ho Yu College and Primary School sends 80 percent of its students to some form of postsecondary education. There are schools in the United States with dedicated staffs who have taken their schools from the ranks of poor performers to much higher performance. But this school made us think. Would our accountability systems tolerate a principal who spent five years building trust in her teachers before turning to academic performance? How many principals of our elementary schools would insist that all teachers specialize and all have bachelor's degrees in the subjects they teach? How many of our elementary school faculties would get upset if the principal tried to lock the doors at 8:30 p.m.? How many local business owners would equip a school in the worst section of town with a biotechnology lab? How many of our schools serving mostly low-income students are sending 80 percent of their students to some form of postsecondary education?

Northbrooks Secondary School, Singapore

Northbrooks Secondary is a regular school mainly serving low-income and minority students. Its motto is "Soaring Yet Rooted," meaning that it intends to help its students achieve great things while being rooted in strong values. The school vision is "Every Brooksian a Champion, Impacting the Community." They want to foster a "strong desire to learn and improve and bounce back in the face of adversity." They want students who "serve by leading and lead by serving." They want a curriculum that fosters a "plethora of deep learning experiences and quality interactions within the school and beyond . . . ."

When we walked into the school, the first classroom we saw was the gym, occupied not by a physical education class, but by students who were launching planes they had designed and built to specifications set by their teacher, who was assisting in the launches and engaging the students in a conversation about each test flight. For this class, the students had been asked to attach weights to their planes at strategic points to put the planes into a stall, from which the plane was supposed to glide to the floor. Some did and others did not, sometimes to spectacular effect. After each flight the teacher asked the whole class why the plane had performed as it did. Both the flight preparations and the conversation after the flight focused on the plane's aerodynamic properties and the way the added weight had changed those properties. The sophistication of the discussion astonished the visitors.

The former principal, Helen Chong, had created not just this class but a whole program in aerospace for the school. No one had told the students that the study of aerospace demanded a level of achievement in mathematics they would never reach. No one had told them that few students with backgrounds like theirs would be able to go on to universities and get degrees in engineering. Chong had reached out to NASA and arranged for the students in her aerospace program to visit the Houston space flight center. We learned that these students were getting the mathematics and science instruction needed to make good on their ambitions.

The aerospace program showed these students that they could do anything they had their hearts set on if they were willing to work hard enough to get there. This idea was reinforced by the rock-climbing wall that Chong had built in the paved playground; that, too, helped them to develop the courage, determination, and belief in self that would enable these students to go the distance.

Chong's approach to these students was built on the same "first the heart, then the head" strategy we had seen in Hong Kong. Win their trust first, and academics set to a high standard could follow. Her teachers, too, had been prepared to go to court to bail out their students if that was what it took to build the trust on which their teaching and their students' learning would later depend. Because her students were seeking the same qualifications that students from more favored families were going for, she, too, did whatever it took to attract great teachers who knew their subjects cold and could teach those subjects at high levels to their students.

The difference between Singapore and Hong Kong, on the one hand, and the United States, on the other, is that the former have developed systems that encourage and support what we have just described, so it becomes what is expected and done everywhere, while we don't have such systems and so have come to view their schools as miracles.

In Singapore, as in Hong Kong, the qualification system structured the curriculum and courses that defined the school's program but still gave the faculty the freedom needed to construct the aeronautics program in a way that engaged students' attention and made them dream great dreams. In this case, as in the Hong Kong case, students' predominantly low-income and minority statuses did not translate into low expectations and a watered-down curriculum because the qualification system set high standards and the supportive instructional system provided schools with an ample supply of first-rate teachers. These schools were no accident, and they are not miracles, either. They are the kinds of schools that well-designed and well-managed systems routinely produce.

Summing Up

The driving idea in this chapter can be summed up very easily: The kind of education we have always provided to the elite must now be provided to everyone. That's because much of the unskilled and semi-skilled work that used to be available to people leaving schools with only the basic skills will be done more reliably and cheaply by digital devices of all kinds. Until recently, the United States could run our schools like a large sorting system, sorting kids into bins labelled for their destinations: unskilled jobs, semi-skilled jobs, skilled crafts and trades, and professional and managerial jobs. The sorting began in 1st grade and continued through the senior year in high school. It was widely thought that only a few students were capable of serious academic achievement, so little was expected of the rest. But that was not perceived as a problem because, except for the skilled craftspeople, most work did not require very much in the way of academic skill or knowledge. Now it is very important that we expect high academic achievement of all our students, whether they will end up as boat builders using advanced carbon fiber technology, farmers controlling driverless tractors from their farm office, or medical technicians implanting tiny sensors in the heart or brain that use radio technology to communicate with devices outside the body.

Now all students will need to have skills and qualities that have always been taught in the prep schools that supplied our future leaders: strong ethical judgement, courage, grit, working independently to a goal, figuring out not just what the solution is but also what the problem is, being a great team member one day and a great leader the next, being a self-starter, having great analysis and synthesis skills, empathy and caring, creativity, imagination, and so on. These skills are profoundly human qualities that intelligent devices will come to late—if ever. Some of these qualities are learned in the classroom, but others are learned on the playing field, in the workplace, or while helping others. Teachers will have to see themselves not so much as imparters of knowledge—though that will still be very important—but as managers of experiences.

When we look at how the top-performing countries are doing this, this is what we see:

1. Time and effort put into building a common vision among the professional and in the wider community, so that virtually everyone is committed to the goal of providing to all the kind and quality of education formerly provided only to a select few and is willing to make the changes needed to get there.

2. Creation of a clear idea of what kind of education all students need to have before they go their separate ways and consensus on when most students should complete that common education (typically by the end of grade 10).

3. Development of a clear curriculum framework with grade ranges and milestones that sets out the trajectory of learning for the common curriculum, important aspects of which are the subjects to be taught, the order in which the component topics in those subjects are to be learned, and the standards to be achieved at each stage.

4. Specification of the qualifications that students can earn as they go through school, each qualification representing satisfactory

completion of the preceding stage and successful acquisition of the knowledge and skills needed to begin the next stage—as one does not proceed to the next stage, in either career or school, without the necessary qualifications.

5. Development of course syllabi, matched to the curriculum framework, that are used by all teachers of the common curriculum and that specify what is to be learned in the course, key material—including books to be used, projects to be undertaken, papers to be written—and how the student will be graded (though not lesson plans, which are to be developed by the teachers, working in teams, in each school).

6. Development of end-of-course examinations and examinations for the qualifications, matched to the standards, frameworks, and syllabi, and accompanied by examples of student work that meet the standards with good grades.

7. Development of techniques for embedded or formative assessment that teachers can use to determine whether the whole class and individual members of the class are grasping what is taught as it is being taught, enabling them to adjust instruction at it is being provided.

When this system is working well, it is set up so that there is more time and support for students who are struggling to master the Common Core curriculum to a global high standard, while more advantaged students get a more enriched curriculum and can move on to get more advanced qualifications earlier. The standards for the qualifications are immovable; the time and support needed to achieve them may be different for different students. It is the very opposite of the sorting system.

What has just been summarized is the approach to the formal core academic curriculum leading to what could be the first qualification, to be reached by most students by the end of grade 10, after which they can choose from among a variety of high school upper-division programs, ranging from a demanding career and technical education program to what amounts to an Associate's degree program in high school to programs like AP, IB, or the Cambridge diploma program. We point out that the currently popular method of designating as Career and Technical Education students those students who take at least three CTE courses in high school would be regarded as a joke in most of the top-performing countries, where CTE qualifications require years of combined classroom study and on-the-job training set to high standards that can only be met by taking very demanding performance examinations. Career and technical education in those countries is not regarded as a dead-end destination for students who struggle in school, because one can get into CTE programs only after demonstrating high competence in the core curriculum.

The instructional system described in this chapter is not just for students who are college bound. It is for everyone and, though it is set to global academic standards, it is designed not for sorting students into different futures, but for enabling all students to achieve high standards. It encompasses not just the head, but the heart and the hand as well. It is about not just what happens in the classroom, but the experiences that students have on the playing field, in the workplace, on field trips, and in the food pantry.

Summing Up: Instructional Systems

Element	Top-Performing Systems	U.S. System
Pathways and Gateways	Qualifications certify that the student is qualified to begin the next stage of his or her education, has passed the performance exams needed to get a "journeyman's" certificate to begin a specified career, or has taken specific required courses designed by the state and earned required grades on externally graded state exams	Diploma is often just an attendance certificate Nowhere does it certify more than an 8th grade level of literacy High school requirements specify time in the seat but do not certify what has been learned or the standard to which it has been mastered

Element	Top-Performing Systems	U.S. System
Academic Standards	Statements of knowledge and skills all students are expected to learn Typically illustrated with examples of student work that meet the standards Typically cover not only native language, mathematics, and science, but also history, social sciences, foreign languages, technology, art, music, and other subjects considered to be in the instructional core	Statements of knowledge and skills all students are expected to learn (e.g., the Common Core for English and mathematics literacy, Next Generation Science Standards) Rarely illustrated with examples of student work that meets the standards
Curriculum Frameworks	Clearly delineated progressions of topics in each subject for entire common curriculum matched to or incorporating the standards Syllabi matched to the progressions that specify the content of each course in the progression, the books to be read, projects to be completed, and how students will be assessed	Sometimes include progression of topics; rarely include required course syllabi; often include teacher-generated curriculum materials that may or may not be reviewed or approved by state authorities and may or may not be usable for full courses or course sequences Many teachers use textbooks as the basis of their curriculum, even though they are not designed for that purpose and may not be aligned with the standards
Assessments	Assessments based on the course syllabi Typically in essay form or performance based, with few if any multiple-choice, computer-scored questions Typically scored by teachers	Rarely designed to assess a particular curriculum or syllabus Mostly multiple-choice, many (e.g., PARCC, SBAC) typically scored by machine

What Can a School Superintendent Do to Create a Powerful, Coherent Instructional System?

If you are a superintendent of schools, and you believe that what we've described in this chapter makes sense, what should you do?

1. Consider creating a Common Core curriculum for all students that could be completed by the end of grade 10 but might not be completed by some students until the end of high school. Consider building that curriculum as the heart of the college-and-career-ready qualification system described here. Let your faculty know that they will be expected to get all but the most severely handicapped students to the college-and-career-ready standard, with a steadily growing proportion of the students reaching that standard by the end of 10th grade, whatever that takes. Let every student know that is your goal for them and that you will not settle for less.

2. If your state has adopted the Common Core, have your best teachers use it to create a curriculum framework that lays out, grade by grade, or grade span by grade span, the order in which the topics specified in the standards are to be taught, culminating in the exams to be given at the end of 10th grade. Note that the mathematics standards in the Common Core include mandatory topics and, at the end of the sequence, additional standards. These additional standards are the standards the authors thought would be appropriate for the last two years of high school, at least for some students. The mandatory standards are those the authors thought all students should meet by the end of 10th grade. You may well find that the Common Core sets a higher end-of-10th-grade standard than would be required to be successful in the first year of your local two-year and four-year colleges, and you will have to decide where to set the standards between these two poles.

3. Once you have set up the curriculum framework, consider using the framework to create course syllabi for your district, defining an explicit set of course designs that will be used throughout the district to implement the standards. You could make these course designs mandatory or advisory, make them advisory for schools in which all or most students are progressing nicely through the curriculum framework and mandatory for schools where that is not the case, or you could set up a school inspection team to visit schools where students are not on a trajectory to success to decide whether any given school is required to use the standard courses. Once you have course designs to implement the Common Core, you will want to create standards, curriculum frameworks, and course syllabi for the more comprehensive core curriculum for which your state may not have any standards. If your district is large enough, you may have all the specialized talent you need to do this. If not, you may want to partner with other districts in your state to get it all done.

4. If your state is using the Common Core, it may be using one of the state consortium tests (PARCC or SBAC) in the grades in which states are required to test (six grades in elementary and middle school and one grade in high school). Those tests will not be matched to your new course designs, but they will be matched to the standards on which the course designs are based. The providers of these tests may or may not have sample prompts for their constructed-response items and may or may not have annotated examples of student responses that earned high marks. They will not have examples of student work for the multiple-choice items and some other computer-generated items. Where you are not able to get these prompts, you might want to create examples of student work that meets the standards and annotations on the work explaining why it meets the standards, and you might want to assemble teams of your best teachers to start developing a suite of standards and associated

materials for every subject in your curriculum, including those subjects for which there are no common standards. Make sure that the examples of student work are authentic, not ginned up for this purpose. Fake work can be identified from a distance, and real student work will earn the support of teachers and students alike.

5. Chapter 6 presents a design for engaging your teachers in a serious effort to develop first-rate lessons and materials to support the instructional system described here. You will need to use the system described in Chapter 6 to curate and populate a growing library of first-rate materials and lessons that your teachers can use to teach the curriculum you are using in your district to get all or almost all your students to your 10th grade standard.

6. The materials your teachers develop should include a wide range of formative evaluation instruments and methods closely keyed to your curriculum. As those resources are being developed, you will want your best teachers to train other teachers on how to use these formative evaluation resources to closely monitor the students for whom they are responsible. The purpose is to catch students who are beginning to fall behind the curve described by the curriculum framework before they have fallen very far at all. The aim is to make sure they never fall far behind. Some testing organizations have developed formative assessment instruments. Some of these instruments are very strong and aligned to the state standards. But others are simply short versions of the end-of-year tests and provide little valuable information for teachers. Look carefully before buying one of these products. Chapter 6 describes a way to organize your schools so that teachers have much more time to work together to design, build, and assess the courses and lessons that will be needed to implement this design. That time will also be available for teachers to work one-on-one and in small groups with students who need extra help to stay on

track. You will also need to make time available before school, after school, on Saturdays, and during the summer to help students who would otherwise fall behind the curve established by the curriculum framework. Even if you do all of this, some students will fall behind, and for them, it is hoped, they will still have their junior and senior years, and perhaps even more time, to meet the standards.

7. When this system is up and running, more and more of your students will be ready, by the end of their sophomore year of high school, to succeed in the first year of community college. If you follow the pattern established by the top-performing countries, you will make the end-of-10th-grade standard the point at which students go in very different directions. Some will go into the International Baccalaureate program. Others will take a full load of Advanced Placement courses or do the Cambridge IGCSE program, all of which prepare students for the most demanding, selective colleges in the world. A much larger proportion of your students will be going in that direction than is the case now because students who meet your 10th grade standard will be ready not just for your local community college and four-year state university, but also to succeed in these very demanding upper secondary school programs. However, many of your students will not want to go down that road. They may want to enroll in a nearby vocational program that provides high-level technical training leading directly to good jobs. Or you might have such a program right in your own district. They might want to enroll in a program for their junior and senior high school years that will result in getting a two-year college degree at the end of their senior year, free of charge. That degree might be in an advanced technical area that leads directly to a good job and a great career or it might lead to transfer to a four-year college for the last two years of a bachelor's degree program. In a system like this, all these options become available.

A Qualification System: Imagine Prep at Surprise

In 2010, the Arizona state legislature passed a law that offered schools the opportunity to try a dramatic new approach to high school education. Instead of offering students diplomas based on time in the seat, the legislation authorized schools to award a Grand Canyon Diploma to students who demonstrated that they have attained the knowledge and skills necessary to be ready for college and careers. Students could reach this level at any point between the end of grade 10 and the end of grade 12; if they did so before the end of grade 12, they could stay in school and take advanced coursework, take dual enrollment courses at a community college, or enroll directly in postsecondary education.

Imagine Prep at Surprise, a charter school in Phoenix serving grades 6–12, took up the challenge. "We were looking for an identity," says the principal, Chris McComb. "We talk about college, career, and life, but what does that mean? This was an opportunity to connect ourselves with something meaningful, and something right to do for kids."

The system Imagine Prep put in place is a qualification system. Such systems are common in high-performing nations but are a radical departure from traditional high schools in the United States. Putting it in place successfully requires rethinking almost every aspect of schooling because students have to hit real performance targets in the core curriculum.

At the heart of a qualification system are the assessments used to determine whether students can demonstrate college and career readiness. Based on NCEE recommendations, which had formed a national network of schools pursuing qualification systems, Imagine chose the examinations developed by Cambridge International Examinations, the organization that develops the International General Certificate of Secondary Education (IGCSE) examinations used in Great Britain to determine students' qualifications for prestigious universities.

The Cambridge program, used by schools in more than 120 countries around the world, offers not only examinations scored by highly trained examiners but also a complete set of course syllabi on which the exams are based. The syllabi are in turn based on carefully constructed curriculum frameworks that step the students through a sequence of topics logically ordered to enable those who work hard to succeed on the exams. The exams are essay based, which means that they can measure kinds of student achievement that are difficult if not impossible to measure with multiple-choice exams. The standards for the courses and exams are internationally benchmarked. Students who do well on the exams are top candidates for admission to the world's leading universities.

To McComb, the examinations defined the system by setting clear expectations for students and enabling the school faculty to build a program of study that would enable students to reach those goals. "The assessments make clear what students need to know and be able to do," he says. "If you start there, you can build back from there to grades 9 and 10."

Unlike many tests used in the United States, the Cambridge examinations truly allowed students to demonstrate their competencies, McComb says. "The exams are short answer, essay format," he adds. "That's different from clicking on an answer that best fits a scenario. Having students express themselves in writing is a better measure of what they are able to do."

Imagine developed an end-of-8th-grade test to be able to place students in high school, so that they would know whether entering 9th graders were ready for the demanding Cambridge program and could help the students who were behind get up to speed. They also created formative assessments to track student progress during the year.

Some of the syllabi were quite detailed, while others were less so. But all of them gave teachers a considerable amount of flexibility, McComb says. "We have early release every Wednesday," he says. "Teachers work in content teams. They work in a four-week teaching cycle. The teachers identify where they want to be, and hold 'data chats' to plan next steps. There is constant adjustment."

The faculty also had to make some adjustments to accommodate state requirements and student schedules. As a public school, Imagine is accountable to the state and administers the state test. The mathematics sequence in the Cambridge syllabus differed from the state sequence, so the school made some changes to that syllabus.

The school also found that the schedule, which had 60-minute periods, was not sufficient for students to learn all of the biology content in the curriculum. So, the school added a "zero period" for students in biology to learn laboratory skills.

Over the years, the school has continued to make adjustments. Data showed that mathematics performance was a problem, so the faculty examined the data and improved teaching strategies. As part of that effort, the school removed a teacher who was ineffective.

McComb is pleased with the progress the school has made. "I still think we have more to do in terms of educating all students on what exactly their goal needs to be, what the Grand Canyon [Diploma] is, why they're in certain courses, and what it means to be proficient in those courses. [But] where we are now versus where we were in 2012—it is a completely different environment."

8. What has been described thus far is a system for organizing a student's academic program that is very much like what you would find in one of the top-performing education systems. In most of the top-performing systems, a student's program encompasses much more than academics. It is, as the American phrase has it, about the "whole person." At the beginning of this chapter, we mentioned that Asian education systems put much more emphasis on developing their students' values and character than we do, at least as an explicit goal. Like the Western countries generally, they are also putting more emphasis on the so-called 21st century skills. In addition to the traditional academic goals, they also put more emphasis on physical development of the student—quite apart from sports—than the Western countries. As we said in our analysis of the effects of intelligent machines on the future of work, all these arenas—the ones that go beyond academics, the ones that touch on our humanity and not just our intellect—are likely to be much more important goals for our students in the future than they have been in the past. What we see in the countries that are furthest ahead is a concerted effort to design schools in which all these goals are fused into a unified vision for student development. This is the implication for you and your school system: As you involve your school faculties and your community in long-range planning for your schools, get them to think with you about schools in which the job of the teacher includes instruction in the usual sense of that term, but goes way beyond that. The job of your school faculties gets reframed as the job of people responsible for creating, organizing, and supervising experiences for students in and out of school, all of which contribute to these expanded goals. Some of these goals will be achieved in your sports program, some in school clubs and activities, some on field trips, some in apprenticeships, and some in the opportunities you create for students to lead other students in and out of school. You offer many of these opportunities now, but most people view them

as ancillary to the main purpose of schooling, which is academics. The idea here is that the purposes of schooling previously thought to be ancillary—values, character, 21st century skills development—have become central. If that is the case, much more attention needs to be given to making sure those opportunities are available to every student and that each student is participating in a pattern of activities that will enable him or her to emerge from school with all the important qualities, not just the academics.

9. The kind of curriculum that is now needed is not the kind of curriculum in which a student can be successful just by paying attention in class, taking good notes, doing the homework, completing the required assignments, and acing the exams. Just as what we used to call vocational education is going to have to be built in the future on a much stronger academic foundation, academic education will have to be much more applied than it has been. As your teachers create your curriculum frameworks, build the syllabi, and craft their lessons, they will have to be thinking constantly about how they can get their students to apply to real-world problems what they are learning, constantly going back and forth between theory and practice. The aim of the whole curriculum is not to enable your students to get their ticket punched, to pass tests. It is to learn a great deal about the world they live in that will be useful to them in myriad ways. This is not a new idea. Alfred North Whitehead, writing in his classic, *The Aims of Education*, once called knowledge that is accumulated but not used "inert" knowledge. He did not think much of inert knowledge. The human brain works by forging connections among its neurons. If those connections are not used, they wither. If you understand something but do not know how to use it, you probably do not understand it. If you want to keep it, you must use it. If you want to learn it at a deeper level, you must use it often and in a more complex way. So our last suggestion to you as you think about building your instructional

system is to think about how your schools can help students make much better connections between thinking and doing.

10. Just as in the case of Singapore, if you set up a system of very demanding standards and a no-less-demanding curriculum, some students will not be able to get any kind of qualification at various gateways. The easiest way to solve this problem is to let these students drop out as soon as the law allows. The next easiest way to address the problem is to assume that these students cannot meet serious standards and give them something to do while waiting for a credential that has no labor market value at all. The hard thing to do is what an increasing number of top performers are doing: finding a way for these students, the ones at the bottom of the heap, to meet the same high standards the other students do, whatever it takes. There are good models in the United States. Make sure that an effective way to meet this challenge is part of your plan.

5

A Surplus of Highly Qualified Teachers? Surely You're Joking!

If the job now is to educate all students to the standards that we previously set for only our elite students, then we have to have great teachers for every student. That seems impossible, at least at a cost that any school system could afford. But it is not impossible. Entire nations have done it. We tell you how in this chapter. We also suggest how school districts can implement strategies the top-performing countries have used, even if their state does not.

In Chapter 4, we argued that how well schools are doing must be measured not against how well they used to do, but rather against how well they have done preparing students for success in a world that is very different from the one we faced when we graduated high school. Teachers in the future will have to provide a deeper and wider understanding of the world and everything in it. They will also have to provide students with a wide range of experiences in and out of school that enable them to acquire the character and values needed in an age in which intelligent digital equipment will do a lot of the work that most high school graduates are qualified to do now.

As you read that, no doubt many of you were thinking, "Where am I supposed to find the teachers who can do what is being described here? It's hard for our best independent schools and the authorities in our most favored school districts to find the kind of teachers who teach in those places. And now you say that we need to educate all our students to the same standard that the students in those schools are now educated to. That will take teachers who are as good or better than the teachers in our best independent and elite public schools. Surely you're joking. Where will the teachers come from?"

There are two answers to this question. One answer is that you can greatly improve the skills of the teachers you already have, which we will address in Chapter 6. The other answer is that you can improve the quality of teachers you are getting from schools of education. That is the subject of this chapter.

Improving the quality of the teachers you hire will seem a very tough slog for many of you, especially since you are likely required to employ teachers who are graduates of accredited teacher education institutions within universities. So, your teachers come from the pool of high school graduates admitted by higher education institutions over which you have no control. Nor do you have control over the preparation those institutions provide. You might conclude that, however frustrated you are with the quality of beginning teachers available to you, there is not much you can do about it, no matter what the top performers are doing to produce a surplus of first-rate teachers. That would be a mistake. There is a lot you can do, but before we get to that, we want to tell you what the top-performing countries are doing. Even though most of what they are doing is through national or state policy, that does not mean it is irrelevant. Bear with us. We will explain at the end of the chapter how you might profit from the strategies the top performers have developed.

How the Status of Teachers Declined over Time

There was a time, in the latter half of the 19th century and the beginning of the 20th century, when teachers were among the best educated people in their communities. For much of that time, few students went beyond elementary school. As the 19th century came to an end and the 20th got under way, secondary education became compulsory, but higher education, like secondary education before it, was only for the elites. So, when the current system was gelling, and our school teachers were required to go to normal schools—which necessitated two years beyond high school—they often ended up with more years of education than all but a few professionals and managers in their towns. Community members looked up to their teachers, even though, as time went on and teaching became a feminized occupation, it was seen as women's work in an age when women's work was not regarded as all that worthy or intellectually demanding.

But then, colleges offering bachelor's degrees were built all over the country, and the teachers, with their two years of education compared to the four years gained by the bachelor's degree holders, were no longer necessarily the best-educated members of their communities. In time, the normal schools became four-year institutions, too. But the former normal schools were widely seen as quite junior in the post-secondary education status hierarchy. Over time, a growing number of professions required a professional degree beyond the bachelor's degree. And a growing number of them had more stringent admissions requirements than the general admissions requirement for the bachelor's degree program in the university of which they were a part. So, step by step, teachers went from being among the best educated in their communities to being engaged in one of the lowest-status occupations requiring a college degree.

As this process played out, the United States was rapidly expanding its public education system. New teachers were demanded in large numbers. Most of the students in the schools would go on to enter the middle class with only modest academic skills. The country did not think it needed highly educated teachers to accomplish that task and saw no reason to pay school teachers what it had to pay its architects, doctors, veterinarians, accountants, and engineers. The status of the school of education kept sinking in the academic hierarchy. Many struggling universities saw an opportunity to offer inexpensive teacher education programs on which they could make a profit that would enable them to support other higher-prestige parts of their operation they would not otherwise be able to support. Some prestigious universities with highly selective colleges kept their small teacher preparation programs, but many got rid of them altogether. Most teachers attended very large public state colleges. Over time, at those institutions, the teachers colleges were widely viewed as the professional schools you could get into if you could not get into any of the other professional schools, because the admissions standards were low and the academic demands on the students modest. Able high school graduates who had strong academic records did not want to go to a professional school widely perceived to be so easy to get into.

There are exceptions to this story: small private colleges that regularly produce strong teachers, major research universities that decided they had an obligation to make an important contribution in this field, high school valedictorians with sterling academic records who were determined to be school teachers. But the exceptions prove the rule.

Despite all this, for a very long time, the United States got much better teachers than it deserved because teaching was one of only a few occupations open to college-educated minorities and women, many of whom are still in our schools. But those restrictions have largely disappeared, and the country is about to reap the consequences of policies that worked once but do not work anymore.

What the Top Performers Are Doing That the U.S. Is Not

When we look at the top-performing countries, we see a different history and a different result. The top performers have built their systems around high-quality teachers; we have built ours around cheap teachers. The top performers, without exception, have made teacher quality a major focus of their effort to greatly improve student performance. All of them have made determined efforts to source their teachers from higher ranges of their graduating high school classes than the United States does. All have moved to raise their standards of admission to the institutions permitted to educate and train their teachers. All have put a lot of emphasis on making sure their teachers have a firm command of both the subjects they teach and the craft of teaching before they get their first job as a teacher. Here we examine each big step in the sourcing and initial education and training of the school faculty, comparing what we see in the top-performing countries to what we see in the United States.

Drawing from a Pool of Top High School Graduates

The first and probably most important factor in determining the quality of your teachers is the quality of high school graduates who decide they want to be teachers. That is the pool from which your teachers come.

The United States gets most of its teachers from the middle of the distribution of high school students who go to college (Goldhaber & Walsh, 2014). By contrast, the top performers get their teachers from the upper ranges of high school graduates. Singapore pulls from the top 30 percent (Stewart, 2010), Finland from the top 25 percent (OECD, 2010), and South Korea draws its primary school teachers from the top 5 percent (Barber & Mourshad, 2007). Canadian high school students who want to be teachers but whose high school academic records are not good enough to get them into a teacher education program in Canada head south of the border to the United States.

When we talk about the middle or top or bottom of the distribution, we are not talking about the same level of academic achievement in each country. Students at the middle of the distribution in many of these countries are performing at about the same level as our top students. The students in their bottom half are performing at or near the level of the students in the middle of our distribution. Put another way, average students who graduate from high school in Shanghai or Japan are likely to have a much better command of mathematics than the average student in our top third. So, when we say that we are mainly getting our teachers from the middle of our distribution and they are getting their teachers from the middle to the top of their distribution, there is a very big difference in those teachers' command of, say, mathematics, science, or history. Because the top performers have exams that put much more emphasis on writing than ours do, their teachers are much better writers. This point will become very important as this story continues.

So, the quality of teachers in the top-performing countries is high both because the general level of high school graduates is much higher and because those countries get their teachers from a higher segment of those graduates than we do. Let's set aside for the moment the fact that the general level of high school achievement is higher in those countries—after all, that is what this whole book is about—and look instead at why the United States gets its teachers from a lower segment of high school graduates than they do. The first reason is that we do not really recruit our teachers at all. If we did, we would go after talented high school graduates by using policy to construct an occupation that is just as attractive as the high-status professions. That is what the top performers do.

But it is not what we do. The United States hires cheap teachers who are poorly trained and do not, on average, stay in the occupation very long (U.S. Department of Education, 2015b). The job is the same on the last day of teaching as it was on the first. Good teachers who need to support a family have to leave the classroom and become managers. When the inevitable shortages of teachers arrive, we waive the already low standards for teachers and give emergency certificates to virtually any college-educated adult willing to stand in front of a classroom, whether or not they know very much about the subject they teach or have mastered the art of teaching it.

When these policies produce poor student performance, we blame our teachers rather than our policies. School teachers tell their own children and their best students not to go into teaching. Applications to schools of education decline. Schools of education, afraid they will be left with empty seats, lower their standards for admission even further, thus accelerating the decline. Does this sound like an occupation that we would like our own children to go into or an occupation that has been designed to attract high-quality high school graduates?

One would think that running a system with cheap teachers would be much less expensive than running a system with well-paid teachers, but it turns out to be very expensive. The international comparative data show that our approach is more expensive than running a system with well-paid teachers. In a system with high-quality teachers, the cost of the constant churn of teachers, which is very high (Haynes, 2014), plummets. Fewer first-rate teachers can do a better job than a larger number of teachers who are not so good, which can save a great deal of money. Better teachers require less supervision and fewer specialist consulting teachers and coaches, which can save even more money. The picture comes into even clearer focus if we look at the relationship between teacher quality and student performance. On balance, American students fall further behind their counterparts in the top-performing countries with every year they stay in school (Mullis, Martin, Foy, & Hooper, 2016; OECD, 2016b). Can we doubt that one of the most important reasons for this is that our teachers were not as well educated as their teachers in school or in college, or as well trained in university, or as well supported in the workplace?

This section began by comparing the pool of high school students from which our future teachers come with the pool from which teachers come in the high-performing countries. We then asked ourselves how the top performers are able to get their teachers from a much better educated pool of high school students. That led us to think about what would make teaching attractive as a career to high school students who could go into high-status fields. The simple answer is decent compensation and a career that is fulfilling and admired. We then established that, in the United States, the pay is low (Allegretto & Mishel, 2016) and the career increasingly unattractive.

Suppose that we wanted a system, like the top performers have, that is based not on cheap teachers but on having highly educated and very well trained professionals in front of all our students, people who are compensated at levels comparable to those enjoyed by people who work in high-status professions and who work in schools that remind one of the environment in which high-status professionals work. What would we have to do to get there?

The story about what the top performers do to make teaching an attractive career is told in Chapter 6. It is a story about higher pay, creating real careers for teaching, and redesigning the way schools are organized and run to make them more like modern professional practices and less like 19th century factories. But it would not by itself change the quality of students admitted to our schools of education and, if that does not change, higher pay and better working conditions will not get us far.

Limiting Admissions to Teacher Preparation Programs

The top performers limit admissions to applicants with very strong academic records, a demonstrated ability to relate to young people, and a passion for teaching. By contrast, we admit into teacher preparation programs almost anyone who can get into a college of almost any quality.

Finland. Many Americans with an interest in elementary or secondary education think of Finland as a country that trusts its teachers. Some have also heard that education is the most admired profession in Finland. By many such measures, teachers have much higher status in Finland than in the United States. And many know that Finland does very well in international comparisons of student achievement (OECD, 2016b). So, many Americans put two and two together and get five. They think that if we just trusted teachers more and gave them higher status in our society, we would have very high performing students. But it is not that simple. Teachers have been highly regarded in Finland for a long time. But student performance has not been that high through all those years.

For many observers, the turning point came in the 1970s, when the Finns began the painful process of closing their teacher education programs and allowing only eight institutions, all of them research universities, to operate programs specifically designed to train teachers in Finland. Candidates for admission to teacher education programs in Finland had to pass a three-hour exam called the VAKAVA, which asks students to analyze and interpret research articles about education. Candidates have six weeks to read the articles before the exam. Prior to that time, Finland had close to 40 teacher education programs. Finland has a population of about 5 million, the size of a typical American state. The typical American state also has in the neighborhood of 40 teacher preparation institutions.[1]

When the Finns did that, they told the teacher education institutions that they had to offer master's degree programs to their teachers, making teacher education and training a five-year program, and they required all future teachers to have a master's degree. At the same time, they told the institutions they needed to offer similar programs (in the interest of equity and alignment), all specified by the state to prepare teachers to teach what the state wanted them to teach. In this way, the teacher education institutions became the linchpins of the larger design for the reform of Finnish education (Hammerness, Ahtiainen, & Sahlberg, 2017).

By limiting the right to offer teacher education programs to research universities, the Finnish government accomplished a number of key goals. First, and probably most important, they changed the first sieve in their teacher supply system from a wide mesh to a fine mesh. From that point on, only those students who could meet the entrance standards of Finland's most selective universities could become teachers. In one stroke, they greatly raised the level of content mastery of the future teachers of Finnish children. Second, they changed the status of teacher education in the minds of the higher education community and the public, thereby raising the status of teachers in Finland. Third, they raised the status of teacher education in the eyes of high school graduates, making teaching a much more attractive occupation for talented high school graduates whose academic achievement made them good candidates for Finland's most selective universities. These were

---

1. The National Council on Teacher Quality estimates 2,000 teacher preparation institutions in the 50 states and the District of Columbia; see http://www.nctq.org/teacherPrep/2016/home.do.

young people who previously would not have considered teaching as a career. Fourth, they raised the standards for instruction of teachers at the postsecondary level. And, fifth, they made it more likely that their future teachers would enter the profession with strong research skills.

University officials in the United States often fear that raising standards for entry into teacher preparation programs will shut off the supply of applicants. That is not what happened in Finland when they limited admissions to teacher preparation programs to their research universities. Many less well prepared students who might have applied before the change in policy no longer chose to apply for admission to those programs. But many very well prepared students who would not have considered applying before these changes now choose to apply. By the very act of raising the standards, Finland had made teaching much more attractive to many of the best of its young people.

This is crucially important, because teachers' salaries do not quite equal the median salary for other workers with the same amount of education in Finland. Not only did the stream of applicants not drop off, but when the system stabilized, 10 young people applied for each available slot in Finland's elementary school teacher education programs. At the University of Helsinki, there were 1,800 applicants for 120 openings in 2013. The number of applicants had grown by 18 percent since 2010. Overall, only one in four applicants for admission into a teacher education program is accepted. In 2016, it was harder to gain entry into the teacher education program (6.8 percent acceptance rate) at the University of Helsinki than the law program (8.3 percent acceptance rate); both programs are among the most highly sought degrees at the university (Hammerness et al., 2017).

The result of these policies is a surplus of first-rate teachers. When we say first-rate teachers, we are not just talking about student performance on Finland's very demanding college entrance examination. The government also requires the institutions to assess applicants' ability to relate to young people and their passion for teaching. They knew very well that people who know their subject cold but who cannot relate well to young people of the age they will teach will not be good teachers, and they also knew that people who go into teaching for the job security but have no real interest in teaching will not be good teachers, no matter how well they know their subject or relate to children. At some institutions, even more is required. At the University of Helsinki, for example, candidates are also interviewed in a group, where they are asked to discuss a teaching scenario. The process helps interviewers judge the candidate's ability to work in teams.

This story is not unique to Finland.

Singapore. There is only one teacher education institution—the National Institute of Education (NIE)—in Singapore, which has a population of about 5.5 million. That institution operates in close cooperation with the Ministry of Education, so that the way teachers are educated and trained, using the Attributes of a 21st Century Teaching Professional framework (see Figure 5.1), aligns closely with

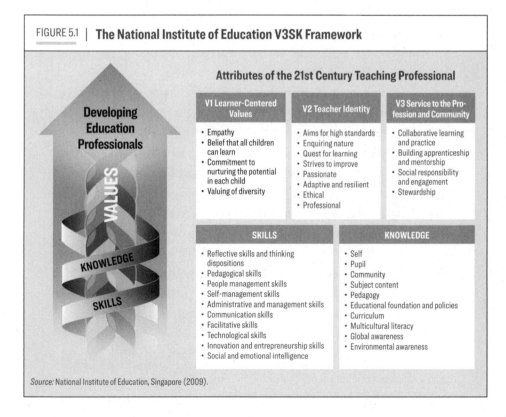

FIGURE 5.1 | **The National Institute of Education V3SK Framework**

Attributes of the 21st Century Teaching Professional

Developing Education Professionals

V1 Learner-Centered Values	V2 Teacher Identity	V3 Service to the Profession and Community
• Empathy • Belief that all children can learn • Commitment to nurturing the potential in each child • Valuing of diversity	• Aims for high standards • Enquiring nature • Quest for learning • Strives to improve • Passionate • Adaptive and resilient • Ethical • Professional	• Collaborative learning and practice • Building apprenticeship and mentorship • Social responsibility and engagement • Stewardship

SKILLS	KNOWLEDGE
• Reflective skills and thinking dispositions • Pedagogical skills • People management skills • Self-management skills • Administrative and management skills • Communication skills • Facilitative skills • Technological skills • Innovation and entrepreneurship skills • Social and emotional intelligence	• Self • Pupil • Community • Subject content • Pedagogy • Educational foundation and policies • Curriculum • Multicultural literacy • Global awareness • Environmental awareness

Source: National Institute of Education, Singapore (2009).

the design and goals of the whole system and with that system's evolving policies. NIE is located in the Nanyang Technological University, one of that country's leading research universities. Applicants to NIE are first screened on their credentials (they must be in the top 25 percent academically), and they must show a genuine interest in children and education. If they pass the required literacy test, they are interviewed. They have to do some demonstration teaching.[2] Only one in eight makes it through these screens (Darling-Hammond, Goodwin, & Low, 2017).

Shanghai. In Shanghai, a metropolis of about 25 million, two institutions dominate the field of teacher preparation. One, Shanghai Normal University, operates as a close partner of the Shanghai Municipal Education Commission. Shanghai Normal is a research university, as is East China Normal University, the other leading teacher education institution. To graduate, prospective mathematics teachers have to demonstrate their mastery of advanced topics in mathematics, like calculus and linear algebra, and have to complete a thesis in mathematics.

Canada. The Ontario Institute for Studies in Education, a world-renowned institution, operates as a close advisor on education to the governments of Ontario and Toronto, the largest province and city in Canada, and provides most of their teachers.

Finland set the pattern, which is now clear. The top performers are moving step by step to greatly raise the standards for teachers, improve their education and training, and attract first-rate young people into teaching by limiting the right to offer teacher education to their research universities. At the same time, they are asserting more control over what those institutions do, in order to bring the education and training they provide into closer alignment with education policy.

Australia may provide the best example of the development of high and thoughtful standards that are influencing a widening range

---

2. See the Singapore Ministry of Education website for information on the application process for teacher training programs, at https://www.moe.gov.sg/careers/teach/teacher-training-schemes/diploma-in-education

of functions that directly affect teacher quality (Burns & McIntyre, 2017). In Australia, schooling is a function of the state and territorial governments, but teacher preparation is a function of the national government, because the national government funds higher education. However, it would be more accurate to say that elementary and secondary education as a whole in Australia is a collaborative enterprise governed by both the national and state and territorial governments. The framework for that collaboration was spelled out in the Melbourne Declaration of 2008, signed by the education ministers of all the education authorities. The cornerstone of the declaration is a commitment to both excellence and equity across the entire country.

These words carried real meaning. Two of the states had high standards for students and teachers but, across the country as a whole, the standards varied widely, just like in the United States. It is no surprise that the whole issue of standards has been front and center since the declaration was issued. An important measure chosen to implement the declaration was the creation of the Australian Institute for Teaching and School Leadership (AITSL). Inspired in part by the National Board for Professional Teaching Standards in the United States, AITSL took the lead in developing consensual standards for teachers and principals. It brought government and representatives of the profession together to analyze the research on teachers' practice and student achievement and come up with agreed-upon standards for teachers and principals: (1) know students and how they learn; (2) know the content and how to teach it; (3) plan for and implement effective teaching and learning; (4) create and maintain supportive learning environments; (5) assess, provide feedback, and report on student learning; (6) engage in professional learning; and (7) engage professionally with colleagues, parents/careers, and the community. AITSL developed detailed versions of these standards appropriate for teachers at each of four career levels: Graduate, Proficient, Highly Accomplished, and Lead.

Having created this system of standards, Australia is using it to determine which higher education institutions are allowed to offer teacher education programs, which students are admitted to them, what level of accomplishment is needed for students to get credit for courses taken in teacher education institutions, which students graduate from them, which students are given provisional certification, which of those who were granted provisional certification get full certification, and then, once the new teachers are certified, which of them go up the developing career ladder in Australian schools and get the salary increases that come with advancement.

Australia is not the only country using standards for purposes like these. There are similar developments in Canada, Singapore, Shanghai, and Finland (Darling-Hammond, Burns et al., 2017).

Requiring Serious Preparation in Content and Craft

We have already established that mastery of the content teachers will teach is typically higher in the top-performing countries than in the United States, both because high school graduates come to college better prepared and because admissions requirements for college and teacher preparation programs are higher in those countries.

But there is more to the story than that. In many of the top-performing countries, teachers must either major or minor in the subjects they will teach, even at the elementary school level. In some of these countries, teachers at the elementary level must specialize in either their native language and social studies or mathematics and science. These teachers must at least minor in the subjects they will teach, taking many graduate-level courses in their chosen subject.

Consider the impact this would have in the United States. In our country, many elementary school teachers have not taken any math or science beyond what they were required to take in high school, did not do well in those courses, don't understand these subjects very well, and have a healthy dislike of both of them. But, because our elementary school teachers teach all the subjects in the elementary school curriculum, they are required to teach those subjects to their students. It should surprise no one that our students do poorly in international comparisons in mathematics and not much better in science. Although not all of the high performers require their elementary school teachers to specialize this way, their teachers are generally better prepared than ours in the content across the board.

The differences in preparation are at least as serious with respect to the craft of teaching as they are for the content. In most of the top-performing countries, aspiring teachers spend five years in higher education before they enter the teaching workforce. Usually, one of those years is spent learning the craft of teaching, which has two aspects. One is learning how to teach the specific subjects the teacher will be responsible for (called pedagogical content knowledge) and the other is the non-content-specific craft knowledge the teacher needs to manage, organize, and deliver instruction to different kinds of students in different kinds of schools.

In a growing number of top-performing countries, schools of education are coupled with public schools in the same way that medical schools operate in relation to teaching hospitals. Whereas this practice has been implemented sporadically in the United States, it has been implemented widely in Finland and has since spread to many of the top-performing countries. University faculty work hand in glove with school faculty to develop, implement, and carefully research new practices, and school faculty in such schools often have faculty rank in the university. Aspiring teachers observe and practice teach in these schools, typically under the watchful mentorship of master teachers.

In countries with student performance standards similar to the Common Core and the Next Generation Science Standards, aspiring teachers are taught how to ensure that students from various backgrounds meet those standards. In countries that have developed curriculum frameworks and course syllabi to match the standards, teachers are taught how to teach those courses to students from many different backgrounds so that they can be successful. The curriculum of the teacher preparation program, in other words, is fully aligned with the program of instruction in the schools. Teachers come prepared to teach the curriculum the schools are using and the students are experiencing.

As teachers in the top-performing countries take on more responsibility for using research and doing their own action research, the universities they attend are giving them the research skills they need to perform these functions well. In Finland, for example, teachers are required to take one course in quantitative research methods and one in qualitative research methods. They must also write both a bachelor's degree thesis and a master's degree thesis that use those skills. Many Finnish teachers go on to get doctoral degrees and continue to teach in Finnish schools.

Other than imparting specific research skills, the instruction in research university-based teacher preparation programs is increasingly focused on helping aspiring teachers to be keen observers and analysts of good teaching. A particularly important aspect of this focus is helping those aspiring teachers to use formative evaluation—that is, evaluation embedded in the teaching itself, on a minute-by-minute, hour-by-hour basis, to figure out which students understand and can use what is being taught, which students do not understand it, and what is interfering with that understanding. Nothing could be more important to the craft of teaching. If the curriculum framework is properly structured and the instruction is well designed and delivered, most students should understand and be able to use what is taught as the instruction is given. But some students will not, for a variety of reasons, understand and be able to use the material. To prevent those students from falling behind, as so many American students do, it is essential that teachers quickly recognize and diagnose the problem and then correct it in real time.

In the face of reported teacher shortages, many U.S. states are waiving the already-low standards that teachers have to meet and are allowing them instead to obtain emergency teaching certificates. This is a time-honored response to teacher shortages in the United States. In this very practical respect, although many states have created professional standards boards to create and enforce standards for teachers, the standards have gone down, not up, as the shortages have worsened.

None of the top-performing countries permit alternative routes into teaching. Some have fifth-year programs for people who decide to go into teaching after being engaged in other occupations. The year is spent learning how to teach a subject they already mastered in college, and they must meet the same standards for subject-matter mastery that every other teacher has to meet. By the time they finish the extra year, they have to meet the same standards for mastering the craft of teaching, too. There are no shortcuts.

Summing Up

This chapter began by stating that it is possible to have a surplus of high-quality teachers. Added to that might have been "at a price that states and districts can afford." With many states experiencing unprecedented teacher shortages, this sounds like a pipe dream. But in this chapter we showed you how the top performers do it.

In other countries, the teacher pipeline starts with the decisions high school students make about what careers they intend to pursue. Historically, when young women with college educations had to choose between being a teacher, a secretary, or a nurse, they often chose teaching because of the job security and the desire to be at home when their children were out of school, giving the schools many top high school graduates simply because more attractive options were closed to female graduates with strong academic records. As a result, schools could attract capable women while paying low salaries and offering working conditions that were hardly comparable to those in the high status professions. Although the options for young women—and minorities— have changed dramatically, the offer has not, which has predictably led to dramatic shortages of teachers.

The strategies of other countries in this arena were very different from ours. While we let teachers' salaries drift down, the top performers were passing legislation requiring that teachers be paid at the same levels as top civil servants and engineers. While the United States continued to let universities at every level of quality offer teacher education and training programs and allowed them to use those programs as cash cows to fund other programs in the university, the top performers were closing down many of those programs and restricting the right to offer teacher training to their research universities. This ensured that their teachers would come only from the ranks of high school graduates admitted to their research universities. They could do this because they were prepared to offer initial compensation and working conditions to teachers comparable to the initial compensation for high-status professions.

The top performers changed the initial preparation of teachers to make sure they have a deep understanding of the subjects they will teach and an equally good grasp of the best ways to teach those subjects. They apprentice prospective and new teachers to master teachers. And, unlike most states in the United States, they do not allow "alternative routes" into teaching that effectively lower the standards for becoming a teacher, nor do they grant emergency waivers in the face of teacher shortages, because they do not have teacher shortages.

The question is what school districts can do about any of this, since they do not control university admissions, decide on university curriculum or programs, or control teacher licensure. From the standpoint of most school districts, the district hiring authorities are pretty much stuck with whatever they can get by way of teacher quality. In the next section, you will find that we have a different view.

Summing Up: Teacher Recruitment and Preparation

Element	Top-Performing Systems	U.S. System
Recruitment of High-Quality High School Graduates	Frequently waive all cost of university prep Some provide salary while still in university Other inducements, including compensation at levels comparable to high-status professions	Little or no effort to recruit high-quality high school graduates

Element	Top-Performing Systems	U.S. System
Admission to Teacher Preparation	Typically limited to those in the upper half of the distribution of high school graduates (in some countries only those admitted to research universities) and those with a passion for teaching and the ability to connect with young people	Open to virtually all who can get into any kind of university, including those with very modest admission standards Typically from the middle of the distribution of high school graduates
Preparation	In most countries, all teachers, including elementary teachers, are expected to take a demanding graduate-level program in subjects to be taught, and to spend at least a year learning the craft of teaching, usually under the supervision of master teachers in close partnerships with schools for clinical experience	Low standards for content preparation, especially in mathematics and science at elementary school level Methods courses often disconnected from subjects to be taught Poor clinical preparation, little or no apprenticeship to master teachers Little connection to schools
Alternate Routes	Virtually none that involves waiving any of the standards for becoming a teacher	Increasingly common; typically involves waiving standards for becoming a teacher

What Can a School Superintendent Do to Build a Corps of High-Quality Teachers?

As stated at the beginning of this chapter, on the face of it there isn't much that school districts can do on their own to build a corps of high-quality teachers. The stories shared in this chapter are all about what state, provincial, and national governments have done to improve teacher quality, not what school districts have done on their own. Some of you will be lucky enough to be in a state in which state authorities have decided to take similar measures. Even where that is not the case, you might be lucky enough to be in the orbit of a university that has been moving in this direction simply because it is the right thing to do.

But the majority of readers will not be in either of those places. So, are you stuck, unable to do very much at all about the quality of the teachers you decide to employ?

We don't think so. School districts typically get their teachers from the same nearby institutions they have always gotten them from. Most teachers in the United States attend a teachers college near where they grew up and then teach in schools not far from the higher education institution they attended. If that pattern is disrupted, more often than not it is because the teacher's spouse got a job offer that he or she could not refuse.

But this pattern is not legislated. No one forces school districts to hire the graduates of local institutions. In fact, large school districts are important customers of the universities that prepare their teachers. Without those customers, the universities would have no students, because no one would want to attend a university that could not place its students. *School districts have enormous market power they very rarely use.*

Leveraging Power to Improve Teacher Preparation

The 24 school districts that make up the Capital Area Intermediate Unit in Pennsylvania had spent two years in the mid-2000s developing curriculum around state standards and preparing teachers in research-based instructional strategies to support the curriculum. But, district leaders found, there was a weak link: new teachers prepared by higher education institutions lacked some of the skills the districts expected all teachers to have. "It came to our attention that student teachers came to us without the background the districts expected of their staffs," said Amy Morton, who was then executive director of the Intermediate Unit.

So the districts banded together and proposed a partnership between the districts and the 19 institutions that provided teacher preparation in the area. "We would tell them what we are doing so they would have an idea of what our needs were," Morton said. "Ultimately, the three biggest providers of teacher candidates were truly engaged in the work."

But the districts also went further. Collectively, the superintendents wrote to the 19 institutions and said that they would not place student teachers in their schools unless the teacher-candidates attended a two-day training to prepare them in standards for instruction. The first year, Morton recalls, 18 of the 19 institutions took the charge seriously. But one did not, and student teachers from that institution were turned away.

Ultimately, the districts and the higher education institutions forged a partnership that continues to this day. The negotiations that led to the agreement were tense at times, Morton recalls. "The teacher prep faculty who attended the initial session sat with their arms folded in the back of the room in a way that was challenging," she says. "It took a little while for them to realize they were better served by a partnership than by finger-pointing."

And the district leaders have not forgotten that they can use their "purchasing power" to strengthen the preparation of teachers for their districts, Morton says. "Superintendents recognized that they were empowered to hold the newest teacher candidates accountable by holding the institutions accountable. People have to realize they can use the power they have in a positive way," she says.

Suppose your district went to the schools of education from which you traditionally get your teachers and said to the dean something like the following:

We've really valued the relationship we've had with you over the years, and you have sent us many good teachers. But we need much better teachers than those we have been hiring for a long time now. We know that, in order to get them, we are going to have to pay them well, offer them real careers in teaching, and redesign our schools to make them more attractive workplaces for young people who could go into the high-status professions. We have a plan for doing that that has been agreed to by the teachers and approved by our school board. We'd be happy to share that plan with you.

What we want to talk with you about is what we need you to do. If you want to continue to send us your graduates, you will have to greatly raise your admissions standards. We'll let you know what they need to be, and we will work with you to develop some screening mechanisms so that you can take into account, in addition to academic accomplishments, candidates' ability to relate to young people and their passion for teaching. If you like, we can help you do that screening. We will need to make sure that your graduates have a really deep understanding of the subjects they are going to teach, much deeper than the people you have been sending us. We want to be sure that everyone you send us has majored in the subject they will teach at the secondary level or, at the elementary level, has at least minored in the subject they will specialize in. Because all our new elementary teachers will specialize in either mathematics and science or English and social studies, we need school programs set up to help them develop that expertise. We would like to work with you to set up a school that will have the same relationship to your own higher education institution that teaching hospitals have to medical schools. We can work together on selecting that school in our district. We want to be sure that the master teachers in that school can get appointments as full clinical professors on your faculty . . . .

You can see where this is going. There's no need to go through the whole litany of what the top-performing countries are doing again. But think about turning our description of what the top-performing countries are doing with respect to preparing their teaching force into a specification of what you would like your schools of education to do for you. Then go sit down with the dean and start the conversation. You are not likely to get everything you want, but you might get enough to make a big difference. After all, they will not want to lose you as a customer. The dean may have been waiting for somebody to do this for years, just because he or she thinks it is the right thing to do and the wave of the future.

If you are the superintendent in a small rural district, you may get nowhere. If that is the case, consider banding together with other like-minded superintendents in the area.

If you make it clear that you will look to other institutions if you are not getting anywhere, and you still get nowhere, then you might want to look somewhere else in the state, to a major university that either has no teacher education program or has a small one that is very good. That might even be the state's flagship university. You might find a president or dean in such an institution who has been waiting for someone like you to walk through the door. Here again, you might want to join forces with other superintendents when you do this.

Then, there is always the state government—the state board of higher education, the top state official for higher education, the secretary of education, or the chair of the House or Senate education committee who has been waiting for just this sort of initiative from the schools to take the lead in making something like this happen.

Our message to you? If you are prepared to play your part by making teaching more attractive as an occupation, you can leverage your district's enormous—and probably unused—market power. The possibilities may surprise you.

All of this assumes that you are doing everything you can inside your district to create strong incentives for highly qualified high school students to go into teaching. Are you prepared to reimburse the cost of their college education completely or to pay off the student loans of the top candidates if they agree to stay on your staff for an agreed-upon period of time? Many of the top performers do this. What about offering the top students a small salary to apprentice in your schools while they are in teachers college, as a way of getting them interested in joining your staff when they graduate? Some of the top performers do this, too. All of this is on top of increasing compensation overall, creating real careers in teaching, and redesigning the way your schools are organized and managed, the subject of the next chapter.

6

Reorganizing Schools
Around Highly Qualified
Professional Teachers

I n Chapter 5, it was argued that the redesign of the instructional system in the United States will fail unless we have first-rate teachers
in front of all of our students, and we have in this book described
the revolution taking place in the top-performing countries. Chapter 5
focused on how to deliver talented and highly trained beginning professionals, on the threshold of their career, for the first day of work as
a salaried teacher. But evidence indicates that, if the revolution stops
there, it will be impossible to attract the kinds of high school graduates
to teaching who are described in Chapter 5 and, even if they do come,
and make it through a teacher preparation program, they will not stay
long in a teaching career.

Most of the teachers who will be teaching in your school 5–10
years from now are already teaching there. You cannot produce the
improvements needed in student performance unless you improve the
teaching skills of your current teachers *and* fully support and make the
best use of the new teachers you will want to hire. That is the subject
of this chapter.

Teachers Lift Up a District by Its Bootstraps

The McComb, Mississippi, school district had a reading problem. Students in the primary grades might be the same age, but their reading levels could be years apart. Giving all the students in the same grade the same instruction was a surefire way to leave some of them far behind. So the district eliminated grade levels in the primary grades and instead provided instruction based on students' reading level. Students might be in a classroom with their agemates, but because one might be two grade levels ahead, and another might be two grade levels behind, they receive very different instruction. It's an equity initiative. The aim is to make sure that all students leave elementary school reading well and ready for the middle school program.

When the district launched the initiative, there was just one problem—McComb's primary-level teachers did not know how to teach this way. The district could have gone out and hired an external consultant to train its primary teachers, but it decided not to do that. Instead, the district asked its principals to identify outstanding teachers, those who have formed what they call the "core of exemplary teachers." These teachers are trained in the new approach and then serve as mentors and trainers for their peers.

"One of the teachers exposed to the new method will roll it out at the school," explains superintendent Cederick L. Ellis Sr. "A teacher familiar with the process will serve as a lead or master teacher at the school, assisting other teachers in grasping the new way of doing things."

In just two years, the initiative has shown impressive results. At the first pilot school, 92.5 percent of third graders passed the gateway test on their first try, up from 60 percent two years before. "If you meet students where they are and provide the right kind of support, students are more comfortable," says Ellis. "We've seen success already."

Ellis predicts that in the long run the core of exemplary teachers will also strengthen teacher quality in the district. "We can retain folks longer by providing them with what they need to be successful in the classroom," he says. "Also, we can recruit teachers who have not traditionally looked to McComb schools, because we can provide the support they need."

Changing the Status of the Teaching Profession

This chapter details how the top-performing countries are transforming the workplace for teachers, changing it from an industrial-era workplace in which teachers are often treated like blue-collar workers into a place that feels much more like the kind of place in which doctors, attorneys, architects, and engineers work. This makes sense for three reasons. First, top high school graduates will not consider teaching as a profession unless they are treated as high-status professionals. Second, the teachers you already have will perform at levels that will surprise you if they are given a modern, professional environment in which to work. Third, the very best new teachers you can get will not be able to do their very best work unless they are working in a place designed to take full advantage of their skill and ability.

Some readers may recoil a bit: "What do you mean by saying that our teachers are treated like blue-collar workers and our schools are not professional workplaces? I don't treat my teachers that way. I am very proud of the way our school district is organized and managed."

We are not trying to stick a finger in your eye here. But we need to give you another perspective on the way your schools are organized and managed. Without that perspective, you are unlikely to seize a giant opportunity to improve your school district's performance. So, bear with us while we review some history that might bring us closer together on this point.

American school administrators may wince at the thought of running schools and school systems on business principles, but our schools have been managed on a strict business model for a century or more, despite mounting evidence that the businesses on which that model was based have long since discarded it. The model of school organization we are about to share with you is based on the business model used by firms that employ large numbers of *professionals*, rather than large numbers of blue-collar workers.

Roots in the Mass-Production Model

The current roles of teachers were framed when they became frontline workers in the industrial era. At the dawn of the 20th century, Ellwood P. Cubberley, the dean of Stanford University's school of education and a highly influential educator, envisioned the school board as akin to the board of directors of a bank and the superintendent as analogous to a business manager. He described schools as "factories in which the raw materials (children) are to be shaped and fashioned into products to meet the various demands of life" (Tyack & Cuban, 1995, p. 114).

Under that model, the managers—superintendents and principals—made the important decisions about how schools would be structured and run, including what should be taught and how it should be taught. Teachers, the workers, would carry out the orders of their superiors in an obedient way. The managers—mostly male—needed more education than the workers—who were mostly female—and were paid considerably more.

A half-century later, Albert Shanker, then a teacher in New York City and later the president of the American Federation of Teachers, described the attitude of his assistant principal: "Be good. Be obedient. Keep your mouth shut. Don't rock the boat. Don't do anything against the administration. Behave." (Kahlenberg, 2007, p. 34). Not much had changed.

Change in the Industrial Workplace but Not in the Schools

But things were changing outside the schools. Forward-looking thinkers began to suggest that this form of organization was becoming anachronistic in business. In 1969, Peter Drucker, perhaps this country's most influential writer on business leadership and management, published *The Age of Discontinuity*, in which he predicted that companies and countries that continued to depend on the mass-production form of work organization were doomed to fail. The firms that would succeed were those that focused on "knowledge work," that is, work based on the production and use of new knowledge. And those firms would succeed only if they employed "knowledge workers," people who functioned not on the familiar blue-collar model but as professionals. This new work, Drucker said, was the kind of work that requires a lot of autonomy on the front line, because new situations would constantly arise requiring expert judgment. Because management could not anticipate what would need to be done at any given moment, management would have to set the goals, hire first-class workers, provide everything the workers would need, measure the results, create the right incentive structures, and then get out of the way, holding the workers accountable for the results but letting them figure out how best to produce those results.

The great wall between management and labor came down and in its place was a world in which the worker often functioned as management in a very flat organization, taking many of the responsibilities formerly assigned to management. In this new model, workers were learning all the time. Learning wasn't something they did when they weren't working. It was woven into the work, an integral part of it. Workers could not do their jobs without researching new ideas and procedures, using statistical methods to figure out what was working and what wasn't and changing course accordingly, learning from the top producers on their teams and teaching them a thing or two at the same time. Even more important, although workers used to rely on the engineers in the upstairs offices to improve the product and how it was made, now the company was relying on the frontline workers to do that. Everyone was a researcher, everyone was learning, all the time.

Transformation in the Top-Performing School Systems

Drucker was describing not just the way the industrial workplace of the 1960s was changing. Though he did not know it, he was also describing how schools and school districts were going to change in the world's leading school systems in the late 20th century, half a century later. The differences between those systems and the United States are stark, especially when it comes to teachers. We describe some of the main differences in the sections that follow.

The Way Time Is Used

In the steel mills a hundred years ago, frontline workers were expected to be on the floor all day long, leaving only for meals and bathroom breaks. Similarly, of all the countries in the OECD database, the United States expects its teachers to be in front of students teaching for more of the day than any other industrialized country (Darling-Hammond, Burns et al., 2017; OECD, 2014b). That is because teachers in the United States have been viewed just like frontline workers in the mill. In those long-ago steel mills, frontline workers were not relied on to make improvements either in the quality of the product or in the efficiency and quality with which it was produced. All the work on the floor was supposed to be directed by people who worked in offices, not on the mill floor. That's where the engineers were, along with the researchers and the others responsible for coming up with improved ways to make steel and to organize the work in the mills.

And that is the way our schools were organized. That is why the United States is home to larger local central district offices than you will find in any of the top performers. In the United States, only about half of the people who work in the public education system work in the schools (U.S. Department of Education, 2017b). We have reason to believe that in top-performing countries, the proportion of educators in schools is much higher. The most important reason this is so is the assumption made a century ago that our teachers wouldn't know very much or have much in the way of skills and would have to be told what to do by the central office staff. Finland, Hong Kong, Singapore, Canada, Japan, South Korea, and the other top performers have made an enormous investment in their teachers so that the expertise needed would be right there in the classroom, and large central offices full of specialized staff and supervisors would not be needed.

For Teacher Expertise, Look in the District

How can school districts improve teaching practice without spending a lot of money? For the Towanda Area School District in Pennsylvania, the answer is use time more efficiently and take advantage of the expertise already in the district.

District leaders agreed that teachers improve their practice if they have time to collaborate. "We studied other countries and found that they teach fewer classes and have more time to work on professional learning," says Amy Martell, the superintendent. "We took a look at our system to see if we could allow that."

Looking at their schedules, the leaders found that their schools exceeded state requirements for instructional time. So they focused on the core curriculum and added time for special classes that provided intensive interventions in reading and mathematics. That freed time to allow teachers to meet regularly.

The district then chose experts in mathematics and English language arts to lead these teacher learning groups. The mathematics department head from the high school will move to the elementary school, where she will coteach two 5th grade and two 6th grade classes and help lead the intensive intervention program. The English department head will do the same.

"They have content knowledge," says Martell. "It will be exciting to see how they work with teachers in a professional learning community. We are excited that they will draw out from them best practices."

The district is asking teachers to determine how much time they need to meet in professional learning communities. "We need to be responsive to what teachers tell us they need," Martell says. "We want to be careful we're not prescribing too much. It has to come from their knowledge of the subject matter and what they need to be collaborative."

"Teacher leaders are underutilized resources in schools."

In the industrial model of schooling, research and development are done in the university and, in big cities, in the central office. In the professional model, much more of the research is done by teachers in the schools, a point we will return to in a moment. In the industrial model, the central office decides what professional development will be needed and engages outside experts to deliver workshops to teachers.

In the professional model, the professionals in the schools decide what kind of development they need and how they will get it. In the industrial model, the central office decides what textbooks will be purchased. In the professional model, schools decide that for themselves.

But if teachers in the top-performing systems are spending less than half their time teaching, what are they doing? And how are they producing higher student achievement than our system, in which teachers spend much more of their time teaching?

With few exceptions, most of which involve supporting students who are struggling academically or personally, most of the time is spent working in teams with other teachers. We'll explain in a moment how these teams are organized, but the point here is that, at any given time, a teacher might be leading a team developing a new lesson in the 9th grade math curriculum, working as a team member on another team assigned to figure out how to make the whole approach to 8th grade integrated science more applied and hands-on, or with another team to analyze the data on student absences to figure out what the problem is and how to address it. As you will see, the meetings of these groups are not talkathons or just an opportunity for teachers to spend time together in "professional learning communities." Each team has a serious, important assignment, with deadlines. Each assignment is expected to result in improvements in student performance. The opportunities for teachers to move ahead in their careers, as you will see, depend in significant measure on the contributions they make, as team leaders and members, to the systematic improvement of their school's performance.

The top performers have discovered that engaging highly competent professional teachers in the systematic improvement of student performance pays large dividends. So large, in fact, that schools in which teachers teach less and work together to systematically improve curriculum and teaching produce much higher student performance than schools like ours, in which teachers teach more and devote much less time to the systematic improvement of curriculum and instruction. Bear in mind, though, that this works only in schools staffed by well-educated and well-trained teachers. Once again, the parts and pieces of this design are well connected.

We can hear you saying that this design is all very well and good, but you could not afford to do this. It would cost too much to employ all the teachers required if your teachers were teaching less than half the time they are now. You've already heard one response to this concern: You would not need to hire many more teachers, at least in large city and suburban districts, because you would need fewer people in the central office. But here's another response: The ratio of students to teachers is usually higher in the top-performing systems (OECD, 2016a). Teachers everywhere would prefer to have fewer students, but the research is clear. Given any particular ratio of students to teachers overall, it is much more effective to have your teachers spend less time in front of students and more time working with other teachers to improve instruction systematically with larger class sizes than to have your teachers spend more time in front of students teaching and less time working collaboratively with other teachers to systematically improve instruction (Darling-Hammond, Burns et al., 2017).

Also, when teachers in the top-performing countries are not teaching class, working with other teachers, or observing them, they are often tutoring students who need extra help. This is a key factor in the ability of these systems to close the performance gap while they are raising average achievement.

Career Tracks

In the steel mill, the workers on the floor, the ones in blue jeans, overalls, and steel-toed boots, did not have careers. The fellow who operated the rolling machine that produced steel bar stock might have that job his whole working life, just like the fellow who operated the crane that took the bars to the storage shed and just like the teacher who has the same job on her last day of work that she had on the first day.

That is less true in the countries with the top-performing education systems. In those systems, a teacher does not have to give up teaching to get more responsibility, authority, status, and compensation. There is a real career in teaching, as in the military, with clear steps in a progression from lieutenant to four-star general or in a law firm from associate to managing partner. In those systems, master teachers in the schools have the same compensation as principals. In the Shanghai system, the position at the top of the schools' career ladder is for a teacher who is so good at teaching and action research that she can earn the rank and all the privileges of full professor in the university, and still be a school teacher.

The Shanghai career ladder has 16 steps, the Singapore ladder fewer. Both are "Y" shaped, starting at the bottom with a position for novice teachers and then advancing step by step to expert teacher and then branching. In Shanghai, there are two branches, one for teachers who want to continue teaching and the other for teachers who want to become school principals and continue from there up to higher positions in management. In Singapore, there is one other branch, for teachers who want to specialize in research or curriculum or some other area and go eventually into district administration and the ministry in specialist roles.

In all such cases, advancement is based on merit, which is assessed against detailed written criteria. As teachers move up the ladder, their principals have an important role in determining who advances, but so do other teachers and key people in the district offices who have had a chance to observe the teachers. At the lower level of the teachers' ladder, a candidate's teaching skill weighs most heavily. Student performance on formal assessments is taken into account but so are many other factors. As the candidate moves up the ladder, the candidate's contribution to the teams he or she has been on will be increasingly important. Moving even further up, after the teacher has been asked to lead some of the less demanding teams or subgroups within a team, the teacher's leadership qualities become increasingly important, as does the teacher's record as a mentor of new teachers and other teachers further down the ladder. It is at this point that the ladder branches. Finally, at the top of the teaching branch of the ladder, the teacher's research production comes to the fore. That will include the papers written and the prominence of the journals publishing them, among other things.

As a teacher moves up these ladders, responsibility, autonomy, status, and compensation increase. In some of these systems, there are certain in-between steps, measured in years of service. That is like the American system, but there is no reward for years of service alone. In this system, there is no penalty for staying on the lower rungs of the ladder.

What we have just described is very like what happens to physicians, architects, accountants, attorneys, and engineers as they make their way from rank novice to a senior position in their hospital, firm, or professional practice.

It is not like what happens to most American teachers. Many of you will add, nor is it what my teacher's union would ever let me do in my district. Mere mention of the phrase "merit pay" is usually enough to stop the conversation. But the reason that phrase stops the conversation is because, in the experience of most American teachers, merit pay is just another way for the boss (read *principal*) to reward loyalists and punish teachers who cause trouble. Or the system is based largely or wholly on cheap standardized tests that do not account for much of what teachers think is important for their students to know and be able to do. Neither system takes into account the contribution the teacher makes to the life of the school and other teachers, nor do they consider the teacher who successfully intercedes with the juvenile justice system on behalf of a student to reverse a judgment that would ruin the life of a 9-year-old.

Among the teachers who see the promise in well-designed career ladder systems is Lily Eskelsen García, the president of the National Education Association, who spoke in favor of the idea at a public meeting convened by NCEE in January 2016 (Long, 2016). Her support for the idea is based on her own experience as a teacher, including many conversations with great teachers who went into school administration but would have stayed in teaching if a system like this had been available to them.

Perhaps the most important benefit of having a career ladder system like this for teachers is to gain the status that comes with proving that one is getting better at the work, just as one gains in status by going up a similar ladder in any other profession. The benefit to the community and the students is the other side of the same coin: It creates a strong incentive for teachers to continually improve in their work. It is a far more effective way to do that than to punish teachers in order to make them work harder.

Who Leads, Who Follows

In the steel mill, it is very clear. The foreman leads, and the workers follow. In our schools, the principal and assistant principals lead, and the teachers are expected to follow. Teachers might be heads of departments in secondary schools, but that role is usually perceived to be largely clerical.

But the division of roles is much more complicated than that in, say, an engineering firm. In any professional services firm the person who leads a team is the person who knows the most about the work. One's position in the management hierarchy is less important than expertise, so leadership roles pop up all over the place, because expertise is everywhere. An individual might be a leader on one project and a team member on another.

So, you might say, doesn't this principle undermine the whole idea of a career ladder? If a teacher can be a leader one day and a follower the next, who needs a ladder? Why not let all teachers be leaders when they want to be? The answer is that not all leaders are equally good at leading, mentoring, or research. You might be comfortable assigning a teacher to lead two other teachers in a short-term task, even though the teacher in the lead does not have the organizational or social skills you would really want in a leader, because that teacher has precisely the subject matter mastery needed to accomplish that task. But you would never put the same teacher in charge of a team of 10 teachers working on a project that you know will likely engage the passions of many members of the team on different sides of important issues. The career ladder not only creates incentives for teachers to get better at the work, but it also is a means to make sure that the faculty members assigned to important roles have the skills needed to be successful.

The Amount of Resources Invested in Induction of New Workers

In the age of mass production, people running machines needed very little skill, compared to the craftsmen who had been needed before; they could be trained to do the job quickly and cheaply. When the current system of schooling was adopted a century ago in the United States, the same model was used. Novice teachers were—and still are—expected to hit the ground running right out of school, without much assistance. But most of their training prepares them poorly for the real challenges of teaching. Many have been told to sink or swim. The result is that new teachers here stay in teaching for one-third to one-half as long as new teachers in the top-performing countries, resulting in nearly constant turnover of neophyte teachers, which has a negative impact on both the school's budget and its students.

Entry Plans: One District's Approach to Supporting New Teachers

When Michele Orner, the superintendent of the Halifax Area School District in Pennsylvania, conducted exit interviews with teachers who decided to leave the district, she realized that the district did not do enough to support new teachers and ensure that they were successful.

"We didn't have a systematic approach to mentor and support teachers who came here," she says. "We could see rookie mistakes, disciplinary problems."

In response, the district developed a plan to strengthen the support it provides to newly hired teachers. This is not an induction program. "I hate that word," Orner says. Instead, it's an "entry plan." Each new teacher will have a mentoring team, consisting of the principal and one or two other faculty members, who will support and guide the new teacher for three years.

"It's all built around a systematic way an individual who is new can become familiar with district policy and practice, strengthen content knowledge and skills, analyze and reflect on their teaching, and develop a professional attitude toward teaching," Orner says. "If you are new to the teaching profession, or someone who comes to us who has taught for a while, these are things we believe anyone needs to be successful."

At the end of each year, the teachers will complete an assessment to demonstrate their knowledge and skills. The first year's assessment will focus on character education, for which their district is known nationally. The topics for the second and third years are yet to be determined. These assessments will provide the district with evidence that teachers have earned tenure, Orner says.

"I recommend teachers for tenure after three years," she says. "How do I know that they are absolutely eligible, and that they earned it? It's more than seat time. How can I be sure that they will be a member of the profession who will make a valuable contribution and impact teaching and learning in the classroom?"

Orner says she hopes the system will encourage people to apply to the small, rural district, which often has trouble attracting well-qualified teachers. "I am hoping that the message I send is, wow, look at the resources—the number of people—who can help me learn and grow."

And, she adds, the system might also help improve teacher preparation. As part of the plan, the mentoring team will sit down with the teacher and his or her university supervisor to discuss what the teacher learned in the preparation program and tailor the entry plan to that teacher's needs. These conversations could help inform the university faculty about the district's expectations and create better alignment between preparation and practice, Orner says.

"Our hope is that we begin to inform the practice that occurs during the university experience," she says. "They will have a better idea of what we expect. I hope that they will partner and become more engaged in what we do here. We often find a disconnect between the university's expectations, in methods courses, and the school system's expectations."

In the top-performing countries, new teachers are given reduced teaching loads for the first one or two years and are assigned to highly expert mentors who are at or near the top of their career ladders. These mentor teachers are relieved of part of their teaching load to take on these novices. The novice teachers observe expert teachers, have their own teaching carefully critiqued by the master teachers, and form a part of teacher teams. They not only learn invaluable lessons about the craft of teaching, but they also learn from their fellow teachers about the values and culture of that school. At the end of the induction period, the supervising mentor teacher has an important role in determining whether the new teacher will be fully licensed to teach. In fact, while the novice is in training, one of the master teacher's important roles is to counsel the novice out of the profession if he or she is not measuring up.

This requires a large investment of time from the most valuable professionals on the school faculty, which is exactly the opposite of prevailing practice in the United States. But the top performers see their teachers as their most valuable resource; to them, investing in the initial development of that staff is not optional.

How Expertise Is Developed

In the steel mill, when a new machine was being installed or a new technique implemented, frontline workers were taken off the line to attend a training in the new machine or technique. All training decisions were made by management; all the workers had to do was show up. That pretty much describes the American system of staff development in schools, except that a fair amount of training is unrelated to any reasonable criterion for what teachers need to know. Many teachers sign up for easy staff development workshops simply to get the credits that will lead to more money in their paychecks.

In the typical professional practice in the United States, such as law and architecture, the professionals are continually monitoring their field, many times a day, for new techniques, new research, new ideas, and new technologies that will help them do their jobs better. Professional development is not something that you do when you are not working at your job. It is woven into the job itself.

In the countries with the best developed forms of modern school organization, the first thing a team does to tackle an assigned problem is conduct a worldwide literature search on the issue. As they research, they might check in with university faculty and independent analysts as well as teachers with expertise they can use. Then they report back to their teammates, and the whole team uses that report to kick off their planning. As they plan, they include an evaluation component, specifying what data they will collect to see how much progress they are making toward their goal and, when they get the data, changing course as necessary. At every step in this process, the members of the team are learning, sometimes at a breakneck pace.

But that is not the only faculty learning that this system is designed to promote. They also frequently learn from one another. Take the development of a new lesson, for example. After the team has done the research we just described and completed their plan, the next step is to develop the lesson, which they do in their team meetings. When the first iteration of the new lesson is done, they will pick one of their members to demonstrate it with a classroom full of students. The team members will be sitting around the edges of the classroom, observing and taking notes. Then the team will gather to critique every detail of the lesson. They will do this for months, making the lesson better and better and tracking the data showing what the students taking that lesson are learning.

Our international research team has watched lessons created in this way and can report that what we saw was simply stunning. In one elementary school in Shanghai serving mostly low-income immigrant workers, we observed a 40-minute lesson in music theory. Among our team members was a graduate of the Curtis Institute of Music in Pennsylvania, one of the foremost music schools in the world. Shaking his head afterward, he said he had never seen anything that could compare to the elegance and clarity of the lesson he had just seen or the degree to which a class anywhere had been able to grasp such complex topics in music so quickly and completely.

The fact is that, in this system, teachers are in each other's classrooms all the time. This activity is so important to the top-performing countries that, in some of their systems, teachers who want to go up the career ladder must log a minimum number of hours every year in other teachers' classrooms, observing their work. This says something about the system's attitude toward teacher expertise. In the United States, we think we need to bring in an "expert"—by definition, not a teacher—to give a workshop on something management thinks is important. According to data from OECD's Teaching and Learning International Survey (TALIS), half of the American teachers surveyed said they had never observed other teachers' classes or provided feedback to them (OECD, 2014b). The view in the top-performing countries is that a lot of the expertise you need is right there in the school in the form of the best teachers in that school. One of the more important criteria for going up the ladder is the degree to which other teachers chose to observe your classroom, because the people who run these systems realized that this is an effective measure of the regard in which they hold other teachers. They visit the classrooms of teachers from whom they think they can learn something valuable.

You can think of these schools in these systems as learning factories, places in which the teachers are learning all the time, like the students, but also like high-status professionals all over the world. The career ladders provide a strong incentive to learn and to keep learning. And the way the school is organized provides multiple ways to learn, from diving into the global research literature to observing first-rate teaching carefully, to correcting course with data on outcomes as an integral part of the development process, to working with a mentor. In the Shanghai system, except for the master teacher, every teacher has a mentor. The message is that no matter how good you are, you can always be better. Which is, as it turns out, no different from the top ballet dancers, actors, and baseball players. Even the best have coaches.

Teacher-Led Professional Learning in Carroll County, Maryland

As superintendent of Carroll County (Maryland) Public Schools, Stephen Guthrie set out to make professional learning in the district more relevant to teachers' needs. In the process, he created opportunities for teachers to take on leadership roles. Teachers stepped up to support their peers.

"When I became superintendent in 2010, I wanted to change how we delivered professional development," he said. "At the time, we had a centralized approach, a standardized way of doing it. During professional development days, we would pull the content teachers out of the building, they would meet with their supervisor, and do professional development based on our system—as opposed to the individual needs of the teachers. I can remember being a teacher in the system. My feeling was, 'I've got to listen to this, even though it may or may not affect me.'"

So he changed the system from a top-down mandate to a bottom-up structure. School improvement teams now meet and conduct a needs assessment, based on a wealth of data. They then develop a plan for professional learning based on that assessment. And teachers lead the professional learning sessions the school team requests. Central office supervisors serve as resources to the schools.

"We've turned it from the central office delivering professional development to teachers deciding what they need and tapping into teachers providing professional development," Guthrie said. "The school decides who delivers PD."

"Carroll County has very good teachers with a lot of untapped skills," he added. "There are lots of experts out there. Teachers are very willing to step forward. If they don't have someone at their school, they can tap someone at another school. Teachers feel empowered."

Guthrie has since moved on to another position in Delaware, but he is full of hopes for the future of the system he created in Carroll County.

Guthrie said he hoped to see the system evolve into a career ladder, and teachers who demonstrate higher levels of knowledge and skill would take on additional responsibilities for leading professional learning—and earn higher pay. But the teachers' union had so far resisted the idea; the union was against the notion of teachers supervising other teachers.

But the system has in some ways developed into a de facto career ladder. Guthrie found that teachers who led professional learning tended to do better when applying for administrative jobs than those who lacked that experience.

"The tell for me is, when I do interviews with teachers who want to be assistant principals, the teachers who had experience beyond their own classrooms did much better," he said. "Those who didn't, their answers are all just about their classrooms. Teachers with opportunities for school impact and county impact had different answers. And by and large, the teachers who got the jobs were the ones who had a countywide perspective."

These systems also provide generous access to professional development in the conventional American forms: workshops. But it goes well beyond that. In both Europe and Asia, government will pay for teachers to visit other countries, sometimes for extended periods, to visit schools, observe classes, talk with officials, and visit universities that train teachers. They are not expecting their teachers to copy what they have seen but rather to be stimulated to think about their own system from a different perspective, taking what they have seen that is useful and adapting it for their own use. This kind of investment in regular classroom teachers is as emblematic of the view that teachers should be treated like professionals as any other feature of the systems we are describing.

How Workers Are Compensated

Speaking of interchangeable parts in the industrial machine, this is a pretty good description of the way frontline workers were compensated in the age of mass industrial production. In the early days of piecework, many industrial workers were compensated on the basis of the number of finished parts they produced in any given time. But, in that system, when the workers produced more in less time, the employers would just reduce the rate, so their employees learned to slow down. They lived longer and got paid the same. As Peter Drucker explains in *The Age of Discontinuity*, the blue-collar worker expected a fair day's pay for a fair day's work, but the knowledge worker expects an extraordinary day's pay for an extraordinary day's work (Drucker, 1969). Blue-collar workers work by the hour. Professionals put in whatever time it takes to get the work done, but they expect that, as they get better at the work, they will be paid more. Teachers in the American system are paid like blue-collar workers. Because of the career ladder system, teachers in a growing number of top-performing countries are paid more as they get better and better at the work, like professionals in any high-status field.

Who Is Accountable to Whom

In the industrial age, it was very clear. The frontline workers were accountable to the foreman, who was accountable to his supervisor, and so on up the chain to the CEO. But in professional service firms, it is more complicated. There are still supervisors, and the people they supervise report to them. But the professionals are also accountable to each other in important ways. In a law firm, if the legal researcher gets the research wrong, the litigator can lose the case. In a hospital emergency room, if the anesthesiologist screws up, it hardly matters what the surgeon does. Legal teams are put together to fight cases, and hospital emergency rooms are home to teams who absolutely depend at every moment on the other team members. Engineering projects are carried out by teams whose members are highly interdependent. In all these cases, everyone knows who is responsible for what and everyone knows who is doing his or her job and who is not. If you are not particularly competent or just plain lazy, everyone knows it and no one wants you on their team. When that happens, your days with the firm are numbered. Sociologists who study organizations call this lateral accountability. The stronger the profession, the more powerful the lateral accountability.

In the schools we have been describing, there is a lot of lateral accountability. If no one wants to observe in your classroom, you are in trouble. If no one wants you on their team, you are in trouble. If you apply for the next step on the ladder and the teachers who are asked about your performance are evasive, you are in trouble. In the kind of school we have been describing, unlike the typical American school, two important things are true. First, everyone knows a lot about the competence of all the teachers, because teachers are in each other's classrooms and on each other's teams all the time. Second, just like the hospital emergency room or the law firm team working a case, everyone on the team depends on all the other members to get the work done. If you don't do your part, my part is in jeopardy.

In a system with strong lateral accountability, the performance of the system is not so dependent on vertical accountability to reach the organization's goals. If you want schools in which all the teachers support weak team members because they are afraid of what the principal will do with unfettered power, then by all means stick with a system in which all the accountability runs from the frontline worker to the supervisor. But if you want schools in which the faculty will work actively to help the principal bring in strong teachers and just as actively to get rid of weak teachers, then you want a system with strong lateral accountability, which is what we have seen in the top-performing systems.

The Way Space Is Used

The operator of the overhead crane in the mill did not need an office any more than the man who shoveled coke into the blast furnace. And we don't give teachers offices, either. After all, isn't their job in the classroom, teaching? But in the top-performing systems, we are beginning to see offices for teachers; after all, the majority of their time is not spent in the front of the classroom, teaching; they are doing many other things, some of which require an office or would greatly benefit from the availability of the kinds of resources typically found in an office.

Teachers in these systems typically meet by grade for at least an hour a week and by subject for an hour a week, among the other teacher meetings they are expected to participate in. In some of these systems, a room the size of a classroom is set aside for the teachers at each grade level. The room is filled with office carrels, in a modern open office setting. Each carrel has a desk, a computer station, a printer, and a phone. The aim is not just to give teachers the most basic of tools available to every other kind of professional but also to create a space that invites conversation among the professionals across that grade, about the students, the curriculum, instruction, or anything else that falls within the arena of their professional responsibility (Darling-Hammond, Burns et al., 2017).

How Poor Performance Is Addressed

In the steel mill, poor performers were fired. After the No Child Left Behind Act was passed in 2001, accountability for principals and teachers carried the same implications. But when the top performers identify a poor performing school, they do not fire the principal or teachers. Under a program called empowered management, the Shanghai education system pairs a low-performing school with a higher-performing school (both schools apply to take part in the program) in order to share expertise and professional learning. One school that took part in the program was the Xiao Tang Primary School. A group of NCEE staff met the principal and staff of Xiao Tang in May 2016, and they described the experience to us. According to the principal, Lu Cuizhen, the school's performance was adequate, but the teachers felt uninspired and the school lacked a coherent mission. The school sought to take part in empowered management and was paired with the Wuning Road Primary School.

Teachers at both schools were eager to be in the program, Lu said. "This school has a lot of young teachers who are very happy to learn," she said, using a cooking analogy to describe their eagerness for new ideas: "If you cook radishes only, they have no taste. If you add more ingredients, that gives it taste." One teacher, in fact, had been on maternity leave when the program started; when she returned, she eagerly sought a mentor from Wuning Road.

Wuning Road teachers, for their part, were eager to share their expertise, Lu said. "Once teachers reach a certain level, they feel their job is not challenging, so this is motivating them to improve." At the same time, the teachers also receive a boost in salary, she noted.

The partnership is intense. A management team from Wuning Road spends three days a week at Xiao Tang School, working with school leaders. Twenty mentors from Wuning Road spend one day a week at Xiao Tang working one-to-one with teachers; the 20 Xiao Tang teachers also spend one day a week at Wuning Road. And a team of expert teachers from Wuning Road provides coaching and professional learning for all Xiao Tang teachers.

The experience has enabled Xiao Tang teachers to observe expert teaching, according to Lu. On one occasion, all teachers from the school got up at 5 a.m. on a winter morning to travel to Wuning Road to observe an English class, she said. "Teachers here didn't have opportunities to observe good classes," she said.

Sometimes the principal of a high-performing school mentors principals of schools not performing so well. Sometimes teachers from a low-performing school are sent to work for a while in a high-performing school and then sent back to help their colleagues learn from their experience. Or teachers from a high-performing school might be asked to work for a while at a school that needs their help. Many other kinds of matchups are used to promote learning within the system. Both the teachers and the principals know that when they are applying for the next step up on the career ladder, their willingness to take on schools, principals, or teachers who need their help will be an important consideration in the judgment on their application, as will the effectiveness of the help they gave when it was needed.

Where the Expertise to Improve the Organization's Performance Is Located

In the steel industry, the technological expertise the company depended on to stay competitive was in the engineers who populated the laboratories, research stations, company development facilities, and research universities, not the relatively uneducated workers on the factory floor. It is much the same in our schools. The big ideas, the latest research, and the evaluations identifying the best practices are all supposed to come from the universities, not-for-profits, and laboratories populated by people with "Ph.D." next to their names.

The top-performing countries have their share of labs, universities, teachers with doctorates, and so on, and many of them are very good, but they also have something we do not have: a large and growing number of teachers who are contributing directly to the knowledge base of effective practice. Shanghai is a leader here, too. As we noted earlier, Shanghai is a leader in organizing its teachers to conduct action research. We refer here not to technically sophisticated statistical research that requires advanced expertise in research methods, but to a form of disciplined inquiry that produces papers on school improvement worthy of publication in refereed journals published by Shanghai's leading universities. According to a national study, 75 percent of teachers in China had published research and 8 percent had published nine or more such papers (Gang, 2010). School faculty get assistance in formulating their action research projects, creating their research designs, and analyzing the data from trained researchers in the district offices of the Shanghai Municipal Education Commission (the provincial school board).

But Shanghai is not alone here. When we talk with Finnish teachers, they tell us that having their teacher training take place in a research university really makes a difference. Aspiring teachers are taught simple research skills as part of their preparation and are expected to use those skills in their work. Many teachers have sophisticated research skills. It is not unusual to find teachers in Finnish schools with doctorates who are doing research that will be published in prestigious journals. The faculty in the schools attached to the major research universities in Finland tell us that they function as a part of the university faculty and as part of the teams that conduct research in these development schools. We hear much the same story in Ontario, where the Ontario Institute for Studies in Education collaborates closely with the Toronto schools and with the Ontario schools more broadly, and in Singapore, where the National Institute of Education trains teachers, encourages and supports teacher research, and has become a major center for world-class education research.

A country in which teachers are seen exclusively as consumers of education research sees its teachers very differently from a country that sees its teachers not just as consumers of education research but also as members of the research community, as people deeply thoughtful and very well informed about their profession who can contribute in an important way to its advancement and therefore to improved student performance. This is just one more indicator of the shift among the top-performing countries toward a paradigm in which teachers are attaining the status of true professionals.

Summing Up

The teacher-leadership responsibilities, professional learning opportunities, school organization, and career ladders in high-performing systems are not isolated policies. Rather, they operate together as a *system* that upends the traditional hierarchical structure of schooling. These systems have numerous advantages.

First, they create strong incentives for teachers to improve their practice, throughout their entire careers. Second, they provide myriad opportunities for teachers to learn, by reading, observing, researching, critiquing, being critiqued, being mentored, mentoring, analyzing their practice, and comparing it to practices near and far—all the time, throughout their day, week, and year. That is what we meant when we said that this model turns the school into a learning factory for both teachers and their students. Third, the result of these systems—when we also take into account the effort these countries make to source their teachers from the upper tiers of graduates, educate and train them in their research universities, hold them to high standards through their whole preparation, and compensate them well—is a highly respected teaching profession, one that capable individuals are eager to join and remain in throughout their careers. By enabling teachers to take on more responsibilities and earn higher pay by demonstrating superior skills and the ability to lead their colleagues' learning, these systems make teaching very attractive.

It is little wonder, then, that high-performing nations have no trouble recruiting and retaining teachers and that these systems regularly produce high levels of student learning. Student achievement is no mystery—it is a function of what teachers and students do in the classroom. Policymakers and education reformers often lose sight of that fact, preferring to focus their attention on other aspects of the system, which may seem more mutable. But as the high-performing countries show, performance can only be as strong as the quality of teachers and teaching in the schools.

Summing Up: Schools as Professional Workplaces

Element	Top-Performing Systems	U.S. System
Time Usage	40 percent in front of children, 60 percent working with other teachers	Nearly all day in front of children
Career Tracks	Clear pathways with greater responsibility, authority, status, and pay based on increasing expertise	Very rare and limited in scope
Teacher Leadership	Common practice	Very rare
Induction for New Teachers	Common, with experienced master teachers as mentors	Rare
Expertise Development	Through teams of teachers working collaboratively	Workshops outside of school, often ineffective
Compensation	Based on expertise and level of responsibility	Based on years of experience and coursework
Accountability	Mainly lateral—to peers	Mainly hierarchical—to administrators
Space Usage	Teachers have offices	Teachers are in classrooms
Poor Performance	Teachers receive coaching and support	Teachers are fired
Location of Expertise	In schools	In universities and central offices

What Can a School Superintendent Do to Reorganize Schools Around Highly Qualified Professional Teachers?

In Chapter 5, we acknowledged that most of the responsibility for the preservice education and training of teachers falls on the universities, not the school systems, and this clearly constrains a school district's ability to reshape the character of the teacher workforce. But we also pointed out that the universities are similarly constrained by the work conditions established by school districts. If the pay is low and the working conditions poor relative to most of the other options that high-performing high school graduates have, they will not choose teaching. In this way, the universities and the schools are joined at the hip. They need to work together so that, as the offer from school districts improves, the universities raise their standards of admission and both work hand in glove to improve the pool from which candidates for teacher education are selected, the education they get in the university, and the resources and incentives for continuing education through their careers.

Here we suggest ways to raise compensation without breaking the bank and show where the money might come from. We also suggest initial moves to reshape working conditions so that they are more attractive to young people making career decisions.

Strengthening Support for New Teachers

Thomas Washington, the superintendent of Crawford Central School District in Pennsylvania, knew the district had a problem: Too many students were struggling in algebra 1, a critical gateway course. And he knew a possible cause of the problem: A number of teachers were new to teaching math and lacked the content knowledge and pedagogical skills to teach effectively.

The problem arose because of a quirk in state law. Teachers who were certified in one subject could earn a certification in another simply by passing a subject-area test. Many did so to protect their jobs at a time when districts were reducing staffs. But this practice meant that a number of math teachers were new to the subject with insufficient knowledge and skills.

Washington's proposed solution was to identify master teachers who could serve as mentors to the novice teachers and help them deepen their content knowledge and pedagogical skills. The details are being worked out, but the idea is for principals to select top-performing teachers—those who consistently get excellent results from students—and have them spend part of the school day working directly with the novice teachers and focusing on instruction, not just on administrative tasks like entering grades, as the state induction program tended to do. Washington says, "A number of teachers are great leaders. They don't necessarily want to be principals, assistant superintendents, or directors of curriculum."

The goal is for the master teachers and the novices to have an ongoing relationship, Washington says. "My idea is that master teachers would mentor folks so they become master teachers."

Ideally, the master teachers could serve other roles as well, such as leading curriculum development and professional learning for veterans. "I'm intrigued by the Singapore model," Washington says. "I don't want teachers to stop teaching. I want them to continue practicing their craft, as well as sharing their expertise with other teachers."

For years to come, most of your workforce will continue to consist of teachers who are already in your schools. Americans are lucky. A great many of our teachers decided on teaching years ago, when options for college-educated women and minorities were few. The result was that we got many first-rate people at bargain-basement prices. Although plenty are leaving, many remain in our workforce. You can limit turnover by creating a different kind of workplace in which teachers are more effective and valued. Much of what follows is designed to help you keep your great teachers and improve the performance of all your teachers, including the ones you already have.

Compensation and Career Ladders

On average, teacher compensation nationwide is near the bottom for people with bachelor's degrees (Allegretto & Mishel, 2016). Without the funds to raise teacher compensation across the board, the alternative is a plan that structures compensation to reward the strongest contributors, to structure the incentives to create an environment in which teachers are always working to get better, and to create incentives for the best teachers to work in the schools serving the students who need them the most.

This is what career ladders are designed to do. They define what it means to be a strong contributor and provide a merit-based (as opposed to loyalty based) system for recognizing strong contributors. They make teaching attractive to people who are willing to work hard but who expect their outstanding contribution to be recognized in advancement and compensation, as in any other profession. If structured properly, career ladders make it possible to identify and support those who can succeed in the leadership tasks that need to be done well for the school to succeed.

Career ladders also enable school districts to use funds that might be available for increasing teacher compensation strategically, by putting most of the new money into the upper reaches of the career ladder.

NCEE is collaborating with the National Board for Professional Teaching Standards (NBPTS) to develop a career ladder system that will issue national certificates based on national standards for teachers, but that will allow districts and states to decide for themselves how to use those certificates (what jobs certificate-holders will be eligible to take on) and how much individuals at each step of the ladder will be paid. It will take a few years to fully develop this system. NCEE and the NBPTS will be looking for partner districts and states to help develop the whole system and to take the lead in implementing it. If you are interested in participating in that process, visit the website of one of these organizations for more information.

Or you might just want to follow the evolution of the system and begin the conversation with your teachers and your union so that you can take advantage of the system when it is launched. That would mean talking about how these systems work in the countries in which they are most fully developed, how you and your teachers might want to adapt such a system to your own circumstances, how the career ladder structure emerging from the NCEE/NBPTS development process might be used in your district, and what the implications might be for the structure of compensation in your district. You might also want to follow developments in your state, since some states will take the lead in adopting this system and there might be an opportunity for your district to participate in the development of state policy and to pioneer implementation in your state.

School Organization and the Use of Time in Your Schools

Start a conversation in your district about the issues raised in this chapter regarding how the work of the school is organized, who does it, who leads it, and how time is used in the school. Create one or more study groups involving the staff and the board. Ask them to read what is written here but also other resources that describe the top-performing systems in more detail and from other perspectives. That will include material about career ladders but much more than that. The references in this book should help you build a reading list.

Once you have organized discussions about these ideas, you will need a strategy for moving forward. Many districts will want all their schools to start doing these things at the same time, but doing so could mean that you are organizing the people who will resist these changes before the potential supporters have shown the skeptics that it works.

You might want to talk with your board about creating incentives for school faculties, principals included, to start moving toward these new forms of school organization. Incentives might include additional funds, but they could also include autonomy from the usual procedures and rules. That could include the right to hire new teachers who meet certain qualifications and outside the usual seniority provisions in many contracts (the union would have to agree to that); the right to structure compensation and the roles of teachers according to a new career ladder structure approved by the union and the board; or the right to restructure the way time is used, so that much more of a teacher's time is spent working in teams and much less time is spent teaching. That way, you could start with the schools that are motivated to move in this direction without unnerving the school faculties that are not yet ready. That might make it easier for the union to support you.

There are lots of places for a district or a school to begin on this agenda. Different schools might want to begin in different places and that should be okay. But you will want to set up the launch to make it easy for the faculties and leaders in the involved schools to exchange ideas and experiences and to get outside help if it is available from people who understand how the modern form of school organization works in the countries in which its implementation is most advanced.

Talk with your local universities about their interest in helping your teachers develop the research skills they need and in starting refereed journals in which they can publish their research. If you have developed the kind of relationships with them that we proposed in Chapter 5, see if they are up for giving your master teachers regular faculty appointments as, in effect, "master craftsmen" of the teaching profession or, to use the language of the day, clinical professorships.

Where to Find the Money

The schools that decide to shift to the new model will want to know (1) where the money is going to come from to fund the increments to the regular salary schedule for each step on the career ladder and (2) how they are going to pay to have their teachers teaching fewer classes so that they can spend more time working together to improve instruction.

There are several places to find this money. One source is federal money now earmarked for professional development of teachers, although the future of this funding is uncertain. But there are two other buckets. The first is your district's professional development budget from other sources. The second is the money you spend on salary increases based on the accumulation of credits for courses taken and certificates earned. In most districts, these buckets, taken together, contain a lot of money.

The evidence for the effectiveness of advanced degrees and certificates is mixed at best. By contrast, the verdict is clear on the effectiveness of credits earned for workshops (TNTP, 2015; Yoon, Duncan, Lee, Scarloss, & Shapley, 2007). It is largely a waste of funds. As we pointed out earlier, the new way to organize and run a school promotes more faculty learning that is far more useful in terms of improved student achievement than today's typical programs of continuing education credits and workshops for teachers. Think about setting up a system that terminates these expenditures for the schools implementing the new design and gives them the money saved to implement the new form of work organization.

If you can get your career ladder system started, at least some of the money you use to fund it can come from the money you now spend on salary increments tied to credits earned for professional development. It would be money far better spent if your aim is to promote useful learning for the faculty. Again, the career ladder, combined with a school organization in which teachers are continually observing each other's classrooms and working together on teams to improve their effectiveness, will produce much more useful learning for teachers than the accumulation of random professional development credits.

Over the longer haul, the district will save the money it now spends because of high turnover rates as more teachers survive their initial baptism and stay in teaching and as more experienced teachers choose not to retire early (like Harriet Minor, from Chapter 1). As the quality of both your current and your new teachers rises, the district should be able to reassign some of the current central office staff to the schools, saving money and giving more autonomy to the schools, which should need less management and fewer expert advisors and specialists.

In Chapter 7, we look at this whole new system through the lens of the equity dimension, asking what the top performers do to make sure that the most vulnerable children can meet the high standards this very demanding system requires them to meet.

7

Equity: How to Close the Gap
When the Bar Is Very High

W e said in Chapter 2 that one could describe the glass representing American schools as half empty if we look at the growing number of countries that are getting better and better results on international assessments while they leave us ever further behind. But if we look at how well our schools have done in the face of the relentless rise in poverty and economic inequality in the United States, then the glass is half full. Although both views have merit, the fact remains that the changing dynamics of the global economy and the steady advance of digital technologies leave us no choice: If we fail to raise average student performance and substantially close the growing gaps in performance as we do so, then large numbers of students now entering kindergarten will face lives of deepening economic struggle.

Much of what you have read so far has to do with what your schools and districts can do to raise average performance dramatically. Along the way, we have pointed to measures you can take that will narrow the gap between the average student and those at the bottom of the performance curve. In this chapter, we pull together the main points we have made about serving these most vulnerable students to help you learn from the top performers about producing greater equity in your system even as you are working hard to raise average performance.

Laying the Foundation—How the Top Performers Deal with Equity from Birth to the Time Children Show Up for Compulsory Education

Most Americans know that the countries of Western Europe have provided strong support for families with young children for half a century or more. Finland, for example, provides an allowance to every family with young children of US$103 per month for every child through the age of 17. This allowance is not means tested. And there is more. In Finland, six-year-olds and low-income four- and five-year-olds have access to free early childhood education, and substantial subsidies are available for others. High-quality child care is free for families with incomes of less than US$36,000, and substantial subsidies are available for families that make more than that. Health care is free for everyone, as is access to child clinics. Professionals make home visits to new mothers. Finnish parents have access to paid time off to take care of newborns and very young children, after which the state-provided child care takes over. In effect, Finnish children are well cared for from the time they are born until they are enrolled in regular compulsory education (Kumpailanen, forthcoming).

What most Americans don't realize is that services for families with young children are growing fast in Asia, too, and similar services are common in places like Canada and Australia. Singapore, for example, provides families with a one-time bonus of US$5,737 for the first new baby and a one-time bonus of US$7,172 for each subsequent child. After the bonus, the government provides US$2,141 per year for each child by way of continuing child support. These payments are not means tested. Singapore has a complex health care system of mandated health care savings accounts into which employers are required to pay, with the result that all families are provided with high-quality health care they can afford. Low-income new mothers are entitled to free home visits from health care workers. Ninety percent of Singapore's four-year-olds and 92 percent of its five-year-olds are enrolled in high-quality early childhood education, subsidized for low-income families. Sixty-three percent of Singapore's three-year-olds are in child care, subsidized for low-income families (Bull & Bautista, forthcoming).

We have provided these details on systems of support in countries with high-performing education systems to make a point. To understand what is going on, you have to recognize two facts about the United States: (1) inequality of income is greater in the United States than in any other industrialized country, and (2) we provide far less support for families with young children than these other countries. That is a devastating combination. It means that our low-income families are poorer and, at the same time, receive less support from the state than do low-income families in countries with superior education systems. Our educators are being asked to shoulder a burden that educators in the countries with the best education systems are not being asked to shoulder.

But the critics who say that our schools should be doing better also have a point. The United States spends more—in many cases much more—per student on elementary and secondary education than all but a tiny handful of other countries (OECD, 2016a). Some of that money is spent on support to children from low-income families to compensate for the lack of support that other governments provide from budgets other than their education budgets. We are speaking here of free and reduced-cost lunches, medical care, dental care, guidance counselors, and other expenses that can be attributed directly to the conditions in which many of our students are living. So extra funds are available to cope with a very challenging situation, but we are still way behind. Socioeconomic status remains a more important factor in determining student achievement in the United States than in a number of high-performing countries (OECD, 2016b). And wide variations exist in student performance among schools serving similar populations of low-income, minority students. These challenges cannot be laid at the feet of society as a whole. Educators need to deal with them.

How the Top Performers Address Challenges Related to Equity

Notwithstanding the fact that many highly industrialized countries do much more for families with young children than the United States does, many of those countries still face serious challenges educating students from low-income and minority backgrounds. They have come up with systematic ways to deal with these challenges that we here in the United States can learn from. In the sections that follow, we compare what the top performers do, versus what we do, once children are enrolled in compulsory school.

School Finance Systems: Fueling Differences in Student Performance Versus Ameliorating Them

The American system of financing schools based on local property wealth fuels inequality in education finance. Wealthy people can congregate with each other to form their own school districts, making it possible for them to raise large sums of money per student with very low tax rates, securing the best teachers and the finest facilities in the state, while low-income families can afford only the cheapest accommodations, leaving them with other poor families, who are subjected to high tax rates that still yield low school budgets. The most important result of this system, however, is not its direct effect on the amount of money available to each school but rather its effect on the composition of the student body. Students in wealthy communities get to go to school surrounded by children from other wealthy families for whom expectations and standards are high and who have myriad connections to adults who can smooth their way to the top, schools in which high academic performance is socially valued. Students attending low-income schools, by contrast, are surrounded by adults with low expectations for the students, an undemanding curriculum, and a social environment in which academic achievement is looked on with suspicion and there are few if any ladders to the top. The result of this system, overall, is that students with the most advantages get the best teachers and have access to the most expensive lab equipment and the most sophisticated technology. Students who have the least get the least qualified teachers and are lucky to have access to any lab equipment or much technology. This is not universally true, however. Some states, such as Delaware, Minnesota, Massachusetts, and New Jersey, have developed funding formulas that do not produce this result, but these states tend to be exceptions to the rule.

The top-performing countries typically do not have school governance systems based on local property taxes. In many cases, the money is raised at the state, provincial, or national level and distributed to the schools at that level by a relatively straightforward formula, which means it is much easier for them to finance their schools in an equitable way. Most now use some variation of what in the United States is called a pupil-weighted system. That is, they start by stipulating a foundation amount for each student and then add standard amounts for students who meet one or more criteria, such as poverty, limited use of the country's official language at home, various handicapping conditions, and so on. In that way, the country makes sure that more resources go to schools serving the most vulnerable students than to others. Most of these countries do not have a suite of categorical programs, one or more for each of these conditions, as we do, so once the money is distributed, the school's faculty has more freedom to determine how best to spend it (Darling-Hammond, Burns et al., 2017).

Who Gets the Most (and the Best) Teachers?

In the United States, the wealthiest communities get the best teachers. When the central cities raise teachers' salaries, the wealthy suburbs raise theirs to preserve their advantage in the teacher labor market. When the central cities invest in raising the skills of their teachers, the wealthy suburbs promptly poach them. Within districts, teachers usually have seniority rights of assignment, so the most experienced teachers can choose to teach in the schools serving students that are easier to teach. The result is that the schools serving the students with the greatest needs typically get the greenest, least experienced teachers, who often burn out quickly and leave the profession for some other field (U.S. Department of Education, 2014).

That is not what we see in the top-performing countries. Many of the top performers allocate teachers separately from the rest of the budget. They are careful to allocate more teachers per student to schools serving vulnerable students than to others. In countries with well-developed career ladders, you will often find the very best teachers serving the most vulnerable students. These teachers are not forced to do this, but the incentives to do so are strong. The authorities have structured the criteria for moving up the career ladder so that it is almost impossible to do so without teaching in multiple schools serving highly vulnerable students along the way. That not only puts very capable teachers in front of highly vulnerable students, but it also steadily increases the number of teachers who have the experience and skills needed to help those students. The same system applies to school principals, with the same results (Darling-Hammond, Burns et al., 2017; Jensen, Downing, & Clark, 2017).

Teacher Leadership Academy: Recognizing Excellence

As an urban district, the Harrisburg (Pennsylvania) School District often has difficulty retaining teachers, because they can earn more money in suburban schools. That was especially true at the beginning of this decade, when the district faced a $22 million deficit and had to lay off teachers, close schools, and cancel a pay raise.

"We put a lot into professional development, but teachers get recruited into suburban districts," says the superintendent, Sybil Knight-Burney. "Other districts provided teachers bonuses. We did not. We're still trying to play catch-up."

The financial situation has improved, but Harrisburg is still unable to provide the salaries the neighboring districts can offer. Knight-Burney and her team decided to find other ways to support teachers and provide a reason for highly skilled veteran teachers to stay.

They began at the hiring process. The school board allowed the district to hire teachers quickly, so they could offer jobs before the other districts. But Knight-Burney wanted to make sure they were hiring teachers who were right for the district and who would be successful. "We want to be able to recruit teachers who are ready to hit the ground running, who have an understanding of what it takes to build strong relationships, improve academic performance of our students, and convince the students that education is important," she says.

To that end, she focuses on their experiences and background. She wants to be sure that they have experience in multicultural and multiracial backgrounds. And she looks at their community service experiences, to determine their passion and dedication. "We want teachers who will stay after school, who aren't looking at the clock," she says. "We want students to see them at a game or concert, or coming to the neighborhood to a church event. Those are the kinds of teachers we are looking for."

Knight-Burney also wanted to do something for outstanding veteran teachers, so she created a Teacher Leadership Academy to provide opportunities for excellent teachers to develop their skills further by observing one another's classrooms, holding book discussions, and engaging in other activities. She got the idea from her own experience, winning a Golden Apple Award as a teacher in Florida. "Golden Apple teachers were treated like professionals," she says. "That's what I wanted to bring to Harrisburg. I created the Teacher Leadership Academy so teachers will feel they mattered."

To create the academy, Knight-Burney pulled together a group of outstanding teacher leaders to serve as a steering committee. The teachers also have a direct connection to the superintendent and can inform her about district policy. Ultimately, though, the academy will be teacher led, Knight-Burney says. "Eventually, I want to work myself out of the equation."

The academy members will serve as teacher leaders in their schools and work with new teachers. They can also participate in a program for aspiring urban leaders the district has started in partnership with Shippensburg University. "Some teachers in the Teacher Leadership Academy want to develop leadership skills but may not want to be administrators," she says.

The district is also exploring a new design for a middle school that will provide new opportunities for teacher leaders. Under the plan, the school will be divided into small learning communities, each led by a teacher. "They will be teachers with a part-time teaching schedule, so they remain in the bargaining unit," Knight-Burney says. "They put together the meetings, work out schedules, set up meetings with parents. The teachers will be empowered to make academic decisions. The Teacher Leadership Academy can provide additional support."

Creating a Diverse Teaching Force

This is a sensitive issue. The literature shows that, everything else being equal, minority students do better in school when they are taught by someone who looks like them. But things are rarely equal (Egalite,

Kisida, & Winters, 2015). Minority students with strong academic records in high school rarely go into teaching, so, as a practical matter, schools often find themselves selecting new teachers with relatively poor academic records to teach in predominantly minority schools. This is a sort of Hobson's choice: Either put a poorly prepared minority teacher in front of minority students or a better prepared teacher who is not from a minority background. That is not what we see happening in the top-performing countries. Shanghai, for example, offers to pay the entire cost of college for high-performing high school students if they agree to work in the schools for five years after they graduate from teachers college and also pays them a small salary while they are in training. This policy attracts strong candidates from all kinds of backgrounds, but it is disproportionately attractive to high school students from low-income backgrounds who need the financial support much more than the students from the wealthier parts of the metropolis. Not only are those students more likely to be poor, but they are also more likely to be the sons and daughters of migrant workers who came to Shanghai from other parts of China and from other ethnic groups (Sato, 2017).

The Teachers College Curriculum

In Canada and Australia, the teachers colleges have courses designed to help future teachers understand the history and culture of the indigenous populations and learn about instructional methods and curriculum designed specifically to help those populations master the same standards that all the other students are expected to achieve (Burns & McIntyre, 2017).

Assistance for Beginning Teachers Serving Vulnerable Students

As we said earlier, it is common practice in the United States to assign novice teachers to particularly vulnerable, often inner-city, students and then provide them little support. That is not what happens in the top-performing countries. In the countries with well-developed career ladders, novice teachers are assigned for one or two years to master teachers to whom they are, in effect, apprenticed. The novices have reduced teaching loads, watch their master teacher do master lessons, observe other teachers and hear their lessons critiqued by experienced teachers, have their own lessons observed and critiqued by their mentor, participate in teachers' curriculum and lesson development groups, and learn about the contributions they will be expected to make to the development of practice in the school. The novice teacher is supported in all these ways. For novice teachers whose first assignment is working in a school serving predominantly vulnerable students, this kind of support can make the difference between floundering and failure, on the one hand, and success, on the other, for both teacher and student (Darling-Hammond, Burns et al., 2017).

A Collaborative System for Helping Struggling Schools

The schools perceived to be failing are overwhelmingly schools that serve low-income, minority children. As you saw earlier in this book, Shanghai has pioneered a system for helping schools in trouble that is, in a way, an extension of the collegial system of modern school organization described earlier. In this approach to improving low-performing schools, effective teachers are paired with less-effective teachers, effective principals with less-effective principals, and effective schools with less-effective schools. The more-effective teachers and principals spend time coaching their less-effective colleagues because doing so is an important criterion for advancement up the career ladder. The less-effective teachers and principals reach out for help because they know they need it, and the people who run the system are more likely to praise them for doing so than to punish them for acknowledging that they need help. This system works. The most important beneficiaries are the low-income and minority students who are most likely to populate the schools that are in the greatest trouble (Xiaoyan, Kidwai, & Zhang, 2016).

Contact Among Teachers and Time to Address Pressing Concerns

As you have seen, schools in the countries using modern methods of school organization typically arrange their schedules so that teachers can meet with the other grade-level teachers for at least an hour a week. Some also set up their schools so that teachers at each grade level share an office space configured to facilitate conversation among the teachers. One of the things that often happens at the regular meetings is a scheduled conversation among all the teachers of a particular student whose performance may be lagging. These teachers pool their knowledge about that student, trying to figure out the source of the problem (for example, whether the student's family was recently evicted, the student is being abused, a parent has been jailed, the student has a problem decoding the words on the page, the student has a fundamental misunderstanding of the way arithmetic works, or some combination of these factors). The teachers work out a plan to help the student and assign responsibilities for executing that plan among themselves. Sometimes the plan involves one-to-one tutoring, which can happen when the teacher involved is not teaching a class. Sometimes it means a slight change in the instructional routine. Sometimes it means a call to the social services provider. This structure, in which teachers teach less and have much more time for a wide range of other duties, benefits vulnerable children especially. In this system, teachers have time, alone or with others, to deal with social services, visit with the family, work up a plan with colleagues to deal with a student's pressing instructional needs, and so on. This is a stark contrast with the American system, in which the teacher only has time to teach (Darling-Hammond, Burns et al., 2017).

A Strong, Structured Instructional System

As you learned in Chapter 4, the top performers have clear, well-structured curriculum frameworks and standard course syllabi that are designed to enable all students to master all course material in the allotted time. The instructional materials are matched to the standard course syllabi. Teachers are trained during their initial teacher training, and during the induction period, to teach these courses to students with very different backgrounds. Thus, the novice teacher in this system arrives not only with strong support from a very capable mentor but also knowing a lot about the course he or she will be expected to teach and how to teach it to the kinds of students he or she has in the classroom (Darling-Hammond, Burns et al., 2017).

The system we are describing was designed to ensure that students from low-income and minority backgrounds could learn at the speed and depth required to keep pace with their cohort all the way through school. In American schools, students often fall a little further behind each year, so that by the time struggling students start high school, they may be three or four years behind their peers.

The typical American practice involves either promoting students regardless of the progress they have made or holding students back for failure to progress, but neither of these practices is effective.

Clarity on What Quality Work Looks Like

We have many times stood in classrooms serving poor and minority students who have said, when looking at a piece of student work that got a good grade in an essay-based examination system, "Oh, if someone had just told me that this is what you wanted, I would have done it." They did not mean they could have done it as soon as they were asked to do it. They meant that, once they knew what the goal was, they were confident that they could have eventually learned how to do it. But without clarity on what quality looks like, they were just guessing at what might earn a high grade. Most of the examination systems in the top-performing countries are essay-based, and most of the examination authorities publish annotated examples of the work that earns high grades on the examinations (Darling-Hammond, Burns et al., 2017). Most American tests do not ask for extended essay-type responses, so it is not possible to show students what good work looks like. The students who are most likely not to know what good work looks like are low-income and minority students, and they would benefit the most from examination systems that produce annotated examples of student work that meets the standards.

"First the Heart, Then the Head"

In Chapter 4, we made the case that in real schools serving real students, many of whom have grown up in appalling circumstances, the faculty must first build trust before they can provide instruction that will make a difference, and this can take years. This obvious truth has important implications. Mechanical accountability systems that impose sanctions on schools and teachers based only on student growth data can destroy the very fabric of trust before it can be built. No top-performing country we have studied has an accountability system that operates this way. Many use student performance data to identify schools that may need help. And many of these countries have inspection teams that then visit the identified schools to see whether there is a problem and, if so, to help the school address it. These judgments are made by highly qualified professionals from outside the school, often including experienced teachers and principals. The key point we made about the schools serving vulnerable students in Hong Kong and Singapore is that they put great effort into earning the trust of their students, building an engaging learning environment, and then educating their students to the same high standards expected of all the other students in those systems. High trust, high expectations, high engagement, and high standards. Those are the hallmarks of the systems that succeed in closing the gap while reaching for very high standards (Tucker, 2011, 2016b).

Summing Up

No single practice accounts for the ability of the top-performing systems to close the gaps between the top-performing students and those at the bottom, between the students from wealthy families and communities and the students who come from struggling families and communities. What is truly powerful is the combination of these measures because, taken together, they are so comprehensive. They cover instruction, the design of the qualification system, the way teachers are sourced and initially trained, the support that beginning teachers receive, the design of the curriculum frameworks, the way the curriculum is adjusted to fit the needs of the most vulnerable students, the kind of assistance provided to struggling schools, and so much more. What it amounts to is a deliberate, determined effort to leave no stone unturned in the search for better ways to support the learning of the most vulnerable students. Much of what is done could not be done without making the key structural changes we have described. The development of clear and detailed curriculum frameworks and course syllabi, the creation of sound career ladders, and fundamental changes in the way teachers' time is used during the school day are only a few examples.

Summing Up: Equity

Element	Top-Performing Systems	U.S. System
School Finance	Schools with students with greatest needs receive more funding	Reliance on property taxes means schools in wealthy communities usually have more resources than students in less wealthy communities
Distribution of Teachers	More teachers—and sometimes the best teachers—assigned to schools with greatest needs	Best teachers get to work in wealthiest districts Within districts, most experienced teachers get to choose schools with easiest-to-teach students Schools with more disadvantaged students do not get more teachers

Element	Top-Performing Systems	U.S. System
Teacher Diversity	Special incentives for minorities with strong academic records to enter teaching State provides instruction to all teachers to help them in teaching minorities	Minority students with strong academic records rarely go into teaching
Induction for New Teachers	Common, with experienced teachers as mentors	Rare
Supporting Struggling Schools	Teachers receive coaching and support from teachers in well-performing schools	Teachers are fired
Addressing Needs of Students Falling Behind	Grade-level teams of teachers meet weekly to discuss problems of students falling behind	Little time or structure for collaboration
Instructional System	Same expectations for all students More support for students falling behind More time for students who need it to get to college-and-career-ready standard	Different expectations for different groups of students Less capable teachers for students who need the most help Less rich curriculum for students who come to school with more restricted experience No extra time for those who need it to get to high standards

What Can a School Superintendent Do to Close the Gaps in Equity?

Consider the following:

1. You and your district will not be in the business of providing families with young children with grants for each child in the family, nor will you be a major provider of child care or in-home care for mothers, but many schools and districts have managed to make a big difference for low-income families by coordinating community services, making it much easier for families to sign up for and receive those services. The Judy Centers in Maryland are particularly good examples of such community centers. This is much less than many developed countries do for their families with young children, but it is still a big help to the low-income families. Many community centers of this sort provide child care services for parents who have few other possibilities for the safe care of their children when they are at work. The same thing is true for less-than-full-day kindergarten and early childhood education programs. In some countries, the same career ladder that covers the regular school staff also covers the early childhood education staff, thereby raising the quality of the experience for the children and raising the status of the teachers at the same time. It may not be possible for you to adopt this feature of a career ladder system for your early childhood staff. Clearly, the more you can do to make sure that your students have adequate medical care, dental care, psychological assistance when they need it, enough to eat, an opportunity to pick up some basic cognitive skills, a place to live, and some love and affection and protection against violence and abuse, the more likely it is that you will be able to help them when they reach your classrooms as regular full-time students.

Union City, New Jersey: No Magic Bullet But Improbable Results

David L. Kirp, a professor of public policy at the University of California, Berkeley, describes most school and district leaders trying to improve their schools as "magpies, taking shiny bits and pieces and gluing them together." It never works, he says. The same people come to the Union City schools in New Jersey "eager for a quick fix. But they're on a fool's errand." What they find instead is the result of a long-term, comprehensive strategy that reaches from preschool to high school. And they see the results of a steady hand on the tiller, pursuing that strategy year after year, as the results get better and better.

In a 2013 book, *Improbable Scholars: The Rebirth of a Great American School System and a Strategy for America's Schools*, Kirp wrote about this urban school district, just outside New York City. It boasts a graduation rate of 89.5 percent and test scores that are at the statewide average (in one of the highest-performing states in the nation). Three-fourths of Union City's graduates go on to college. The number of Union City graduates going to top universities like Yale and MIT went from 8 in 1997 to 73 in 2001.

What's improbable about this story is the student population. The community is poor, with an unemployment rate 60 percent higher than the national average. Three-fourths of the students come from homes where English is not the primary language.

The district did not get there by pursuing the most popular "reforms" of the last quarter-century. "The district has not followed the herd by closing schools or giving the boot to hordes of allegedly malingering teachers or solicited Teach for America recruits . . . . Not a single charter has opened there," Kirp tells us.

Instead, what Union City has done is "so obvious, so tried and true, that it verges on platitude," he writes. "Indeed, everything that is happening in Union City should be familiar to any educator with a pulse."

It may have been obvious, but it is too rarely done. Tom Highton, the superintendent, and Fred Carrigg, executive director for academic programs, ended up with a strategy that mirrors many of the principles underlying the success of the countries with the top education systems.

They put more financial resources behind students who are harder to educate than students from more fortunate backgrounds. They created a strong system of early childhood education that assures that students begin formal schooling ready for the program offered in the 1st grade. They worked hard to raise expectations for student achievement to high levels. They developed instructional systems that include curriculum frameworks that prescribe what topics will be studied in all the core subjects in the curriculum—grade by grade—from kindergarten through high school, making sure that school faculty have the training and support they need to provide the instruction needed by the students to progress at the rate called for by curriculum framework. They created an environment in which teachers are treated like professionals and are expected to collaborate with one another to continually improve the outcomes for students. Finally, they worked overtime to weld all the elements of the system into a coherent whole.

According to Diane Curtis, writing for Edutopia, Carrigg "gives the majority of the credit for the transformation of Union City to the teachers who finally got a say in how to educate children. Too often, he says, teachers are 'handcuffed and not given the opportunity to be the professionals they are . . . .'"

2. There is probably little you can do about the way school funds are distributed in your state. But you can do a lot about how they are distributed within your school district. Think about whether you want to distribute all the money that goes to the schools using a pupil-weighted formula, with a base amount for each enrolled student and an additional amount for each student with a number of possible characteristics such as an indicator for poverty, mother's education level, non-English speaking, special education, and so on. Once the student body of each school is analyzed in this way, that school would be free to use the money as they wish, but they would be accountable for their success in producing the highest possible average student achievement and the smallest possible gaps in performance between the most and least successful students.

3. How you distribute your teachers really matters. Like many of the top performers, you might want to distribute your teachers using the same weights that you use for the pupil-weighted distribution of funds. When you do that, you might want to take into account not just the number of teachers but also their cost,

which takes into account experience and expertise, not just head count.

4. How you distribute all the other resources available to your schools also matters. You might consider making public the value of all the resources that go to each school, not just the cost of the teachers. Districts that do the research needed to address this question often discover they are spending much more on schools serving relatively well-to-do students than on those that serve students from impoverished backgrounds.

5. Offer incentives for your best teachers to serve in the schools that need them the most. Think about using your new career ladder system to structure these incentives.

6. Use some of your budget to subsidize, in whole or in part, top high school students in college if they will contract to teach in the schools serving your neediest students when they get their license to teach. Offer them the chance to apprentice to your best teachers when they are in college and in their first year or two on your staff.

7. Work with the institutions that supply most of your teachers to help them design courses to help prospective teachers understand the vulnerable children in your system—who they are, what their lives are like, their outlook on life and their future, how to make contact with people who are influential in their community, the people in the agencies that serve this population, and the myriad other things that will help them understand their students, gain their confidence, and help them. Offer to help the university design the curriculum for these courses and to find instructors to deliver the courses to prospective teachers.

8. When you are building your career ladders and implementing them, make sure that you set aside a significant amount of time for your master teachers to thoroughly mentor your novice teachers, especially the ones you will assign to the most vulnerable students. Make sure those students get enough time and the right kind of supervision to observe and talk with expert teachers

of vulnerable students, have an opportunity to teach such students while being critiqued by expert teachers, and participate on teams with senior teachers who are playing important roles in building effective lessons and improving the instruction of your most vulnerable students.

9. Set up a system for identifying schools that are failing to provide to vulnerable students the opportunities they need to succeed. When you have identified them, set up partnerships between successful principals and those who are in trouble, between successful teachers and those who need their help, and between successful schools and those schools that could learn from them. Use your new career ladder system to provide incentives for the successful principals, teachers, and schools to help those who need that help. Set up an inspectorate of some sort to monitor progress and correct course for the principals, teachers, and schools identified as needing this kind of help.

10. When you change the way time is used in your schools and allocate much more time for teachers to work together, make sure that, among the things that take place in the weekly grade-level meetings, there is time and a process dedicated to identifying students in danger of falling behind and collectively building a plan for dealing with the problem, whatever that takes.

11. As you redesign your instructional system along the lines described in this chapter, ask some of your best teachers to gather authentic examples of student work that meets the standards and annotate them so that everyone who looks at them knows just why the examiners gave them good grades. Make sure that the students, teachers, and even parents have them.

12. Make sure that you have a curriculum framework that realistically steps the student through the months and years from the first day in school to the last day of 10th grade in steps that provide enough time for the most vulnerable students to keep up. Then make sure your staff has the knowledge and skill not only to deliver the curriculum but also to quickly identify students

who are falling behind and provide the on-the-spot and real-time help the student needs to succeed. The whole system should be set up so that every elementary school student arrives in middle school ready for the middle school curriculum and every middle school graduate arrives at the beginning of 9th grade ready for high school-level work. That goal should be the heart and soul of the new system. It is the key to real equity.

13. When you put your new qualification system in place, with the new college-and-career-ready qualification at its heart, make it crystal clear to everyone that the first and most important obligation of every teacher in the system is to make sure that every student who is not severely handicapped is on track to get that qualification, no matter what it takes, from the first day of kindergarten to the day the qualification is awarded. Set up your data systems to make sure the data needed at every step along the way are available to everyone who needs them to do their part. Make sure your accountability system is set up first and foremost to track student progress toward the qualification and to reward—through the career ladder system—faculty who contribute to student progress toward attaining the qualification, particularly the most vulnerable students' progress.

8

Leading the Revolution: From the Bottom, the Middle, and the Top

Many years ago, an MIT professor named Douglas McGregor described what he called Theory X and Theory Y (McGregor, 1960, 1967). Theory X was meant to describe a theory of management based on motivations consisting of extrinsic rewards and punishments. This was the theory—implicit or explicit— on which the management of frontline, blue-collar workers in the mass-production factory was based. Theory Y was a theory of motivation based on intrinsic rewards. McGregor argued that psychological research demonstrated that Theory Y not only worked but was much more effective than Theory X. According to McGregor, once a worker's most basic needs had been met, what was most important to him was a degree of control over his own fate, self-respect, using and increasing his talents, responsibility, status, recognition, and a sense of personal development and effective problem solving. Theory Y was the view taken of modern professionals: eager to learn and contribute, full of expertise that needed only encouragement to flower and produce the results that management wanted to achieve.

McGregor was making a case for abandoning the factory model of management in favor of a professional model. Though his observations are a half century old, they remain pertinent to the current environment in public education. Yesterday's factory managers would have been very much at home with the punitive accountability systems introduced with the No Child Left Behind Act, which are essentially founded on the principles of Theory X. The countries with the best-performing education systems have been much more comfortable operating on the assumptions of Theory Y. For them, leadership development is largely a matter of developing leaders who have the outlook framed by Theory Y and the skills needed to manage in a way that is consistent with that theory.

This is important because the revolution described in the preceding chapters cannot and will not happen without leadership in the schools, the central office, and the superintendent's office that is committed to Theory Y and to the development of the kind of system we have described. In that sense, leadership development is the key to implementing the entire agenda that flows from this book.

Getting All the Leaders on the Same Page Is Crucial

Most of the literature on leadership is about school leadership, not school system leadership, but this perspective is much too limited if the aim is to implement the agenda at the heart of this book. It's useless to help individual principals see the challenges facing them and to give them the tools they need to get much better results if, after receiving that training, they return to a district with a central office staff and a superintendent whose view of the goals and the best way of achieving them are framed by Theory X. If you want a whole district and schools within it to operate very differently, you will need to align the leadership from top to bottom around a new set of goals and a new way of achieving them.

At the beginning of this book, we recalled the position of the leading manufacturing firms in the United States when they were surpassed by Japanese firms that had adopted the policies and practices advocated by American quality gurus. The American firms, threatened with extinction, hired consulting firms to help them develop entirely new goals and strategies for achieving them. They realized that those goals, plans, and strategies had no value unless they were able to get them out of headquarters and into the heads and hearts of every manager at every level of the firm.

Before then, human resources or personnel had been a minor player in the corporate hierarchy. Suddenly, it became player number one. Everything depended on executive development. Giant corporations invented the corporate university to get the job done and to continue indefinitely to induct new executives and update others. The CEO and board chair became a lead instructor within his or her corporate university. Jack Welsh, then the CEO and board chair at GE, visited the GE corporate university at Crotonville, New York, at least once a month to lecture to his colleagues. He was not alone among corporate chiefs (Tucker & Codding, 2002).

These giant corporations adopted a change strategy based on leadership development because they were not just introducing a new technology or product line but a whole new way of thinking that needed to suffuse the entire organization and everyone in it. That is exactly what is happening now in the countries with the best-performing education systems. They have come to the same conclusions about implementation strategy that the corporate manufacturing titans came to more than 30 years ago. This book ends with a chapter on leadership because the evidence suggests that if you, too, want to run your education system along the lines now used by the top performers and use strategies aligned with those principles, you, too, will need a leadership training strategy to get there and you will need to make sure that all your leaders are on the same page.

Training Principals to Run Successful Schools in a Dysfunctional Education System Versus Training Them to Lead the Implementation of a High-Performance System

The context in which the top-performing countries developed their leadership strategies is quite different from the context for leadership development in the United States. The mass-production approach to manufacturing and to industrial organization was invented in this country and had a more profound effect on the development of our schools and school district organization than it did elsewhere. The top performers introduced compulsory secondary school after the mass-production era, while we developed it in the midst of that era, a big reason why that form of industrial organization had a larger effect on our schools than it did on theirs. We built larger schools and larger and more complex district organizations than other industrial countries. Our schools were headed by principals who ceased to teach. Their schools were headed by head teachers who continued to teach. Our principals were relied on to manage schools under the direct supervision of central office executives who were expected to have more management expertise than the principals, who were treated more like factory foremen than the headmasters in the schools of other countries. Our principals were kept on a relatively short tether, while their headmasters had much more autonomy. Our teachers were expected to be in the classroom teaching almost all the time, while the principal ran the show, but theirs spent more of their time with the head in a kind of collegium in which the head was practically equal to the others.

One consequence of this early history of schools in the modern era is that, in the United States, much more than elsewhere, principals came to be seen as managers and teachers were more or less left alone to teach as they wished. Principals were not selected for their knowledge of teaching and learning, but for their skill in school administration. That began to change in the 1970s with the research on effective schools. That research produced lists of characteristics of principals who ran these effective schools, especially in areas serving disadvantaged students. The lists described principals who were 10 feet tall, excellent school administrators who also excelled at creating a compelling vision for the school, enlisting everyone who moved in executing that vision and who knew more about reading than the English teachers and more about science than the science teachers. This 10-foot-tall person had the moral stature to fight off all the evils of modern inner-city politics and the political and bureaucratic skills needed to outfox the barons of the central office. No one had any idea how to create such people.

The era of leadership defined by the lists associated with the "effective schools" movement gave way to the imperatives of the "principal as instructional leader" and the idea of "distributed leadership." Neither idea was new. The idea of principal as instructional leader had dominated the principalship of head teachers in other countries for a hundred years or more. But it was made possible there by much smaller schools and a much smaller central office, which meant there was no bureaucracy above the school expecting the principal to be an administrator first and an instructional leader second, if ever. Some opined that the job really required both a manager and an instructional leader in two separate positions, but this did not happen because it would have required adding administrators and diluting the principal's authority. The idea of the head of an organization delegating some of his or her responsibility to others in subordinate positions is as old as the hills, but who was the principal going to delegate all this authority to when the teachers were teaching all the time and no one was about to add a new gaggle of executive positions to the school staff? As a result, neither of these ideas went very far.

Then came the accountability movement. For the first time, student performance was at the top of the agenda. But the principals had not been hired on the basis of their expert knowledge of how students learn or the best methods of teaching them. They had been hired for their ability to competently administer a complex organization operating in a highly political environment. No one took away any of these expectations. The authorities just added responsibility for assuring high levels of student performance and for rapidly increasing the rate of improvement in student performance. The reforms failed to produce improvements in student performance, but they did produce a substantial shortage of people willing to be school principals.

In retrospect, the outcome we just described was inevitable in the light of everything outlined earlier in this book. Think about the situation in which Harriet Minor found herself (described in Chapter 1). She had a good set of student performance standards, but she and her colleagues, expected to teach practically every minute of the school day, had no time to turn them into well-designed curriculum frameworks, course syllabi, or lesson plans. The tests used to hold her accountable did not match the standards to which she was supposed to be teaching. The materials available to teach the courses were not aligned to the standards or the nonexistent syllabi. Because there was no career ladder, there was no structure of teacher leadership available to lead the teacher teams that might have been assigned to deal with these enormous challenges. But that did not matter because, even if there had been a good distributed leadership structure, there would have been no money and no teacher time available during the school day to get the work done.

You cannot get your school leaders to greatly improve student outcomes by telling them they will be fired if they don't. You cannot get them to do a better job just by training them to do the things that industry managers are expected to do. It works in industry because the training is designed to fit these systems. The top-performing countries, however, have been redesigning their systems and then training their managers to effectively implement those new systems. We, by contrast, have been trying to train our managers to produce miracles in a system that was designed a century ago for a different world. The key is taking a lesson from the top performers and training educators to implement a new system.

Leadership Development for High-Performance Systems

In 1999, NCEE got a call from Michael Levine and Vivien Stewart at Carnegie Corporation of New York, asking if we would be interested in designing and building what they called a "national war college for school principals." The call followed a meeting involving Carnegie, the Ford Foundation, and the U.S. Department of Education. The participants had different education reform agendas, but they were united in their belief that, if nothing were done about school principals, neither their agendas nor anyone else's would get very far. Applicants for principals' positions were declining and serving principals were retiring at earlier ages. Fewer and fewer people, it seemed, wanted the job. The schools and districts serving predominantly vulnerable students were the ones in the deepest trouble. The participants in the meeting saw no sign that the leading universities were going to change the situation. So Carnegie decided to call us.

We thoroughly researched the leading training programs for school administrators in the United States and found nothing on which we thought we could build. We engaged one of the world's leading researchers on school administration to do a scan of school leadership training worldwide, and he came to the same conclusion. A growing number of countries were redesigning their entire systems along the lines described in this book, but they had not yet focused on school leadership as such, largely because they viewed their school heads as head teachers. Then we commissioned studies of leadership training in other fields. The two that seemed more promising were the military and business.

We spent a day at the National War College in Washington, D.C., with three provosts, one current and two prior, talking about how the lessons learned by the world's leading military leadership development institution might apply to the world of elementary and secondary education. The provosts, after listening to us describe the organizational structure of the school systems, concluded that they could not help us. The schools lacked the career ladder system on which the military relied to provide incentives to military officers to keep learning and growing on the job and the clear criteria on which career advancement depended.

We then focused on what we could learn from the business world. The innovative American business model that helped leadership right down to the shop floor understand the goal and rationale for their new direction, as well as the specific role each executive and manager would play, struck us as the right model. After all, we said to ourselves, the task for American schools and districts was very much the same as the one these companies faced: how to produce much better results with no increase in cost.

The next question we faced was how to do the training that needed to be done. We spent a day at the Harvard Business School with the assistant dean for technology. We never left his office. HBS, perhaps the world's leading business school, was figuring out whether the new information technologies could improve instruction in their famous Master's in business administration program. The program is case-based. HBS was spending about $800,000 to create each case. Then it was spending $1,000,000 to convert the printed case into a fully interactive version for real-time instruction (Marc Tucker, unpublished field notes, 2001). The result: MBA candidates who took the course in their rooms connected to the professor by an intranet, and using all the digital tools that HBS had created to augment the lecture, learned a good deal more and retained it longer than the students who sat in the classroom with the same professor.

We developed a blended model for the development of serving school principals: part digital delivery and part face-to-face instruction, all delivered over a 12- to 15-month period. We would develop a small group of people certified to a high standard who could in turn develop the principals, using our curriculum in a face-to-face environment, supplemented with digital delivery. We hired John Fryer, a former commandant of the National War College, and Bob Hughes, who had been dean of the National War College when Fryer was commandant, to run the program. Hughes, who would go on to run the National Institute for School Leadership (NISL) when Fryer left, brought, among many other things, an unparalleled grasp of the importance of strategic thinking in leadership.

We engaged the former director of the MIT Sloan School of Management's Executive Development Program, Marie Eiter, to help us think through a curriculum that would incorporate the best work being done in the training and development of serving business executives (Eiter, 2002). On her advice, we organized our program around a set of key dimensions of leadership she had identified from the literature: leader as strategic thinker, leader as driver of change, leader as having a teachable point of view, leader as coach, leader as creator of culture, leader as decision maker, and leader as driver of results. Our director of research, Peter Hill, one of the leading educational researchers in Australia, brought an encyclopedic grasp of the research literature on education to match the literature on leadership to create a curriculum based on both. The leadership literature and the education literature were married to the research on adult learning, which stressed the point that adults come to learning experiences of this sort with a great deal of experience on which they can build and that they can share. They are not a blank slate on which to write. Finally, we also built on the experiences of the best universities and military and business leadership organizations with a methodology that heavily emphasized the case method, simulations, games, and action learning projects.

Two years and $12 million later, we had the kernel of our first offering, an executive development program for serving school principals. Our first big break came when David Driscoll, then the commissioner of education for the Commonwealth of Massachusetts, decided to use NISL's executive development program in implementing the massive education reforms that Massachusetts had adopted in the 1990s. Then Pennsylvania adopted the executive development program statewide. Other states soon followed, with Minnesota, Missouri, and Louisiana choosing NISL as a key component of their strategies to support school leaders at scale. In time, the executive development program became the largest single program for developing serving school principals in the United States.

Powering this steady expansion were independent evaluations of the program. When we started, we never imagined we would be able to show a direct link between the training of principals and student performance. But we were wrong. A series of quasi-experimental designs used by researchers at Johns Hopkins University, Old Dominion University, and others consistently showed statistically significant gains for students in schools headed by principals trained in the NISL executive development program (Nunnery, Yen, & Ross, 2011; Nunnery et al., 2011). We were, frankly, astounded.

We were certainly surprised that there was any statistically significant effect on students, not least because of the cost. The cost of the specific version of the training in the evaluation just described varies according to the number of trainers we train at any given time. But in the most common configuration, the cost per principal trained is $8,560. If you divide that number by the number of students in the average school in the United States, that works out to a cost of $16.58 per student. It is not easy to come up with a long list of interventions that will produce statistically significant effects for students at a cost of $16.58 per student.

According to a research study conducted by Johns Hopkins University and Old Dominion University in 2011, the students in 38 elementary and middle schools led by NISL-trained principals gained more than a month in additional learning than the students in the comparison schools. The effect sizes were .14 in mathematics and .11 in English language arts—about the same as ability grouping and problem-based learning (Nunnery et al., 2011). We had developed a highly cost-effective education reform.

Early in the second decade of the 21st century, however, we realized that, successful as it was, two very important things were missing from the NISL model. First, the principals we were developing were going back into systems in which neither the superintendents nor the other central office executives had been developed. The more effective the development, the more likely the principals were to be frustrated when they tried to implement their new ideas in a system still in the grip of the old ways of doing things. We needed a system design that could get the whole leadership structure in the district on the same page, much as the corporate universities had done for the companies that invented them.

Second, although the NISL curriculum incorporated the best ideas worldwide from leadership development in business and the military, and relied on the best research on education in the United States, it was not based on what NCEE had learned about the strategies used by the countries with the most successful education systems. Over the years, we had learned, as you have seen, that their success was the result not of the adoption of a set of discrete and separate policies and practices, but of a new model that had its own shape and integrity. The policies and practices were so successful precisely because they were embedded in that model and were much less successful when they were adopted without the rest of the new system in place. It was the shape of this system that was coming into focus as the most important element in the success of these top-performing countries.

In 2015, we went back and began to redesign the NISL program to deal with these two realities. We fully updated the material related to the best research on leadership worldwide. We did the same for the education research.

There were two big changes. The first was that we fully incorporated what we had learned about the strategies used by the top-performing countries to build world-class education systems as we restructured the curriculum. The second was that instead of just focusing on serving principals, we reimagined the program as providing a nested set of trainings.

One program is for cohorts of school superintendents, providing the knowledge and skills needed by a superintendent to lead his or her district in a redesign process that would incorporate everything we had learned about designing and running highly successful education systems. The program relies heavily on the case study methodology using complex examples of problems of practice that tease out nuances and force superintendents to explore issues of quality and equity in their own context and requires each superintendent to take on a real project and implement it, a project based on one of the nine building blocks of a world-class education system (Tucker, 2016a). Superintendents often partner with other superintendents in the group who are focused on a similar project so that they have a sounding board and thought partner.

The second program is for a single superintendent and his or her executive team. The curriculum is similar to that in the first program, but the applied learning project is likely to encompass a larger swath of the nine building blocks and is intended to enable the district both to develop the necessary knowledge and skills to build a world-class system and to take the initial steps in putting what they are learning into practice in a supported environment.

The third program is a redesigned executive development program for school principals, this time with the nine building blocks used as the framework for the curriculum.

We have begun the design of a fourth program, for teachers who want to acquire the skills needed to move up a career ladder of the kind described in this book.

This suite of offerings is designed so that an individual could first encounter this whole agenda in a training designed just for superintendents, top district officials, principals, or teachers, but could then join forces with others in a district so that in time all the leaders at every level of the district are on the same page, working in a common framework with shared goals and a shared set of strategies for achieving those goals.

That is exactly what we see happening in the top-performing countries. The main difference between the original NISL executive development program and the new suite of training programs is that the new version is oriented toward a design for building high-performance education systems derived from close to 30 years of studying the world's best-performing education systems. Those systems have not stood still. In the intervening period, several of them have focused on the training of their school and system leaders as a key part of their implementation strategy for the whole design.

When we undertook this redesign of the NISL program, we went back to Marie Eiter and asked her to tell us what had changed in the literature on leadership since we had asked her to survey that literature more than 15 years earlier. Two things emerged from that analysis. The first was the idea of the leader as developer of talent. According to this idea, which we had first heard years earlier from the provosts of the War College, one of the most important roles of leaders is to develop the pool from which the next set of leaders would be chosen at every level. The idea had emerged from the shadows into the sunlight in the business world. We thought it was high time for the same idea to emerge from the shadows in the education world as it clearly had in the top-performing countries.

The second response from Eiter was that the idea of the leader as a driver of change needed to be broader to reflect the fact that the environment is changing continually. In the world of business, the new mantra had become VUCA, or volatility, uncertainty, complexity, and ambiguity. These four words seemed to neatly sum up the world in which education leaders increasingly functioned and in which they would have to lead. Helping education leaders become developers of talent and to function at a high level in a VUCA environment seemed to be worthwhile goals, in addition to the ones we had been pursuing (Eiter, 2015).

In the end, we found ourselves combining the leadership development curriculum we had been perfecting over more than 15 years with the structure provided by the nine building blocks of a world-class education system, with its focus on effective systems and system thinking, to build a program intended to develop leaders who could bring the new-model system to life. It would be built on the idea of leader as designer, builder, and mobilizer of the new system.

The Top Performers Now See Leadership Development as a Keystone of Their Designs for High-Performance Systems

While we were in the midst of redesigning our own leadership development program, we asked Ben Jensen to research and analyze the leadership development programs in the top-performing countries, to make sure we were incorporating their most important features in our design. It turned out that we were. Here is how Jensen summarized the elements of high-quality principal preparation programs (Jensen et al., 2017):

- They emerge from a national or provincial strategy for how schools should be led to prepare students to be successful in the future.
- The role they prepare principals for reflects a national or provincial design for how schools should be organized or managed, which includes leadership roles for teachers in the schools.
- They rely on mentoring of new principals by highly effective and seasoned school leaders who are selected and trained for this role.
- They require participants to design and carry out action learning projects focused on real problems in their or another school and they evaluate the participants on these projects.
- They follow up with continued networking and learning opportunities for cohorts of new principals who have gone through the program.

Singapore

When we look at Singapore, for example, what we see is a system for training school leaders that does exactly that. It does not just train school leaders in generic management and leadership, nor does it just expose them to the best of the education research literature worldwide. It is designed to prepare them to lead in a specific kind of environment, an environment based on Douglas MacGregor's Theory Y and Peter Drucker's conception of knowledge workers and knowledge work. It is built around the idea that modern education systems have to be built on first-rate teachers sourced from the upper reaches of their high school classes, trained in a research university, equipped with research skills, and prepared to work in a high-performance work organization in which they have a career that looks very much like the career structure for other high-status professions. The principals in the Singapore system are expected to create and run schools that look like the schools described in the preceding chapters.

This is a key point. Just as the teachers are not just taught general principles of good teaching but are taught how to teach the specific courses the students will be expected to take, the principals are taught how to run schools designed on the principles that have been described in this book, the principles that drive their own systems. They learn how to identify and groom potential leaders as they guide them deliberately through a series of assignments meant to develop their capacity as leaders. They learn how to develop the teachers who want to go the master teacher route. They learn what it means to be an instructional leader in a school in which many teachers are the leading experts in their school in the subjects in which they specialize. They learn how to develop and improve the master schedule in a school in which most of a teacher's time is spent not in the classroom but in meeting with other teachers. They learn how to run a school in which merit and not favoritism governs the principal's relationship with the faculty. In these and many other ways, they learn the specifics of managing teachers who are to be treated as professionals, in schools that have been redesigned specifically for that purpose.

In the years since Carnegie Corporation first asked us to build a national war college for principals, the top performers have moved from just assuming that their head teacher–principals would be able to do whatever was necessary to lead their schools through the revolution we have been describing, in which they have created career ladders for school leaders, a curriculum for their development, standards for assessing whether they are ready to move on to the next rung on the ladder, and assessments for certifying their standing on the ladder. Interestingly, when Singapore started to develop such a system, it looked to the American military for a structure to use as a starting place for their design. In a way, they retraced the steps we had gone through to create NISL. But they were able to go further. This whole model of training is made much more powerful when it is lodged in a career ladder system, because school leaders then have a strong incentive to acquire the needed skills.

Australia, Shanghai, and Other Countries

Singapore is not the only country that has seized on a leadership development strategy for implementing the revolutionary design at the heart of this book. Australia's Institute for Teaching and School Leadership (AITSL) is essentially a new national institution tasked with creating standards for teachers and school leaders fashioned into a career ladder that can be used to drive their continuing development system nationwide. Shanghai has a similar system and indeed pioneered the use of a career ladder system to drive it (Zhang et al., 2016). Many other countries have come to see that the systems they are creating require very different kinds of leaders and leadership than the systems that preceded them, indeed that the new systems will not succeed without a new style of leadership. They have also come to see leadership development as necessary to drive their systems to the next stage of development. Finally, they have come to see that they will fail if they do not get all their leaders, from the top of their system to the bottom, on the same page as their own education systems go through successive transformations.

The Limits of the District Model for Education System Transformation

In the Preface, we said that we wrote this book for superintendents of schools and their staffs, though we hoped it would be read by many others, including state-level policymakers. We did that, we said, because we are convinced that local districts do not have to wait until the policymakers in their states adopt the agenda presented in this book before they can take action on their own, working in concert with their school board, parents, and community.

But it would certainly be much easier for a local school district to adopt and implement an agenda like this if the state was fully behind it and willing to create a supportive policy environment. That will be the subject of our next book.

The American governmental system for education is a double-edged sword. In most high-performing countries, it is quite clear where the buck stops—that is, which level of government has the primary responsibility for the overall health and effectiveness of the elementary and secondary education system. In the United States, that has become less clear with each passing decade, with each level of government vying for control over key functions. From one perspective, this is a serious problem, because it makes it exceptionally hard for the United States to develop highly effective system designs when myriad actors, none of whom report to each other, and most of whom are pursuing different visions, claim control over vital functions. That is the downside.

On the upside, our highly fractionated system provides lots of opportunities for those whose motto is *carpe diem* ("seize the day"). In most states, the very looseness of our system, its lack of the kind of structures found in many other countries, creates opportunities for those at the local level with a clear vision of how to create the kind of system we have described here. If enough of you do that, it will become the new system. Just as the states are often called the laboratories of democracy, local cities, towns, and school districts are the laboratories of the states. You might be surprised at how little stands in the way of engaging your community in the design of a new-generation system and how much support you will get when you raise that banner.

The Pivotal Role of Leadership at the Local Level—Getting Started

We started this book by laying out a challenge that can be met only by a fundamental transformation of the American education *system*. We put the emphasis in that sentence on the last word: *system*. We said the new-model system would have to be built not just on new policies and practices, but on new principles. Those principles include abandoning the idea of the system as sorter of students and embracing the idea of getting all but the most severely handicapped students to very high standards of achievement; abandoning a system built on cheap teachers treated like blue-collar workers for a model built on highly capable, well-educated, and well-trained teachers sourced from among our best high school graduates; and thinking about schools not as places in which students go to classes to be taught, but as places offering a full range of learning experiences in and out of class designed to produce students who leave high school with the cognitive achievements, social skills, moral character, work habits, and knowledge needed to survive and prosper in a world being reshaped by digital technology almost beyond recognition. Employing such teachers to create this sort of learning environment would require a complete rethinking of how schools are organized, how teachers' time is used, and even how physical space is arranged in a school. It would mean rethinking school finance, how planning is done, and the school's role in supporting the healthy development of very young children even before they arrive at the schoolhouse door. And it would require completely rethinking what we used to call vocational education to build a form of applied learning intended for students who can do academics but prefer to learn by continually putting their new ideas and knowledge to work in a practical world.

Not only did we cast an image of a world transformed in all these ways, driven by a unified set of principles, but we also said that one of the most important properties of this system would have to be its coherence, the way all its parts and pieces fit together, within the district and within the school.

When we put it that way, it should be crystal clear why leadership is so important to the outcome and why it is no less important that all the leaders in your system be on the same page.

Leaders, Start Your Engines . . . !

Here are some ideas about how you might get started:

1. This book has covered a lot of territory at a brisk pace, and it has presented a radical argument for transformational change. Without the book in hand, could you make that argument against others who have very different views? The place to begin is with yourself, to make sure you really do understand, agree with, and are able to defend the views presented here. Select some of the publications listed in the Bibliography in areas where your own knowledge is a little sparse and dig into them. You may do that and come to different conclusions than we have and that is fine. What is really important is that you emerge from this learning with a deeper understanding of the context for your work and the outlines of an analysis and a plan that you can defend against all comers.

2. Start thinking about how you might engage your stakeholders in taking the same journey you have taken, wrestling with the same issues, reading the same sources, arguing about the same things. Remember that the countries that have made the biggest and most rewarding changes in their education systems have not shortchanged this stage of development. They have erred on the side of being inclusive; gotten a wide swath of views, making sure everyone had the facts and not just opinions; found a way to help everyone understand the underlying forces that are reshaping the world their children will grow up in; and given them a concrete sense of goals that the countries that are furthest ahead have set for themselves and the strategies that the top performers have been pursuing. Involving all these people in this way is the only way to build a shared vision that will stand the test of time and serve as a durable north star for the work ahead. This is a marathon, not a sprint.

3. Create a planning process directly based on the analysis and vision that not only does the things just described but also produces a plan that is coherent, set to high standards, and likely to lead to both high average performance and real equity, a plan that will have strong backing from all the important quarters and

includes an implementation plan to which the implementers are committed.

4. Your plan does not need to cover all the details for years ahead, nor does it need to cover all of the building blocks of high-performance systems in equal detail at the outset. It needs to include a broad framework that can shape the work on all of the building blocks for years to come, as well as a carefully chosen small set of initiatives with which to begin the work. Choose some that will result in easy wins that will earn you permission to take more difficult steps later. Choose others because you will not be able to make later moves until these things are in place first. As you lay out your steps, think strategically. You want to build support as you go, step by step, rather than organize your enemies and disperse your friends.

5. Think hard about the core building blocks of your new system, each one in your own specific context. What will you do to start the ball rolling on increasing your supply of first-class teachers? Is there a university leader with whom you can make common cause? A state legislator who might be interested in creating the legislative basis of a career ladder system for teachers and school leaders? A chief state school officer who might work with you and other superintendents to go from where the state is to the kind of cohesive, powerful instructional system described in Chapter 4? If you have thought long and hard about your long-term plan, you can then step back and select opportunities to get started that present themselves in the shape of allies in key positions to move key parts of your agenda for you or in partnership with you. That goes for partners inside and outside the school system. The best way to start is where you have the best opportunities on which you can build later, as long as the strategy you choose is aligned with your strategic aims.

6. Make sure all of your leaders, at every level of the system, are on board with your plan and have the capacity and incentives to play their assigned roles in the plan's implementation. The

implementation plan should be included in the plan itself, and be sure to ask the people who will lead implementation of particular parts of your plan to write those parts of the plan.

7. Don't fall into the trap of thinking that it is all about you. It isn't. It is about building a steadily expanding base of support for the plan from a steadily increasing number of people who own the design and execution of the plan they helped develop. But don't settle for a half-baked plan or a half-baked implementation of the plan. You will need to hold everyone's feet to the fire.

8. Put as much effort as you possibly can into building a steadily expanding staff of first-rate teachers and first-rate leaders. Nothing you do is more likely to bring success. Nothing else you do will work unless you do this. Find the very best you can find wherever you have to go to get them, persuade them to come to your system, apprentice them to the best people on your staff, and then support them in every way you can, including by giving them a succession of carefully chosen assignments as you help them to develop their capacities over time.

9. Find a university you can partner with, led by someone—probably a dean—who shares your vision and is prepared to meet you at least halfway. The model for that relationship is described in Chapter 5. There are lots of different ways to get there. The main thing is to be in agreement with your partner on the path to be taken.

10. Don't lose sight of the state of your instructional system and your opportunities for strengthening it in all the ways described in this book. Putting your qualification system in place, for example, is, by itself, a large undertaking. Developing a mindset in your system that it is the job of every staff member to make sure every student who is not severely handicapped is expected to gain the college-and-career-ready qualification—most of them by the end of grade 10—will require a transformation in thinking. So, too, will the idea that every teacher is personally responsible for knowing whether every student is on track to reach the

qualification by the end of grade 10, and that it is the responsibility of all the teachers of any given student to pool their knowledge of each student and to figure out what to do if that student starts to fall behind. Focusing like a laser on these key components of your high-performance system will also get you a long way down the road.

11. Redesigning schools in the image of the model described in this book will take time. It will probably require extensive conversations with your teachers and your principals. The roles of both will have to change a lot. The key is the new career ladder system. But the reallocation of time and the way it is used will be transformational, too. There will be many issues about how the teachers and other professionals currently on your staff will fit into the structure you propose to build. If you choose to connect with the national career ladder development program described in Chapter 6, you will get support for this work. If you don't, you may be able to get support from your state department of education.

12. The journey will be long and full of unexpected turns. In one of the states in which we are now working, our sponsor is the state association of school superintendents. That makes it much easier for the superintendents who are in training with each other to partner with one another as they start to put their training to work in their own districts. You might want to gauge your association's interest in working together on this agenda, with the association supporting its members as they work together to transform their districts in the ways described in this book.

13. The preceding suggestion leads inevitably to this one. Sooner or later, you and your colleagues among the superintendents in the state will find that your path would be a lot smoother if you had the right legislative and regulatory framework in place at the state level. You may wish to work together with other like-minded superintendents to seek the legislative and regulatory changes needed to align the state's policies with this agenda.

If the superintendents were to make common cause with the school boards, the principals, and the teachers, it would be hard to resist.

14. Finally, never forget that your role is chief designer, the person whose job is to envision and bring into being a modern system for modern times, a system whose parts and pieces have to work in harmony, a high-performance system that can deliver the very high average performance with real equity that the best-performing systems in the world are delivering. Design is a mindset and an orientation, very different from the mindset and orientation of the person who conceives of herself as doing her best to make the current system work for as many people as possible. Yes, you have to do that, too. But the aim is not to keep the lid on. The aim is breakthrough performance.

Summing Up

Nothing about this agenda is easy. There will be obstacles everywhere. But overwhelming evidence from the top-performing countries indicates that when this agenda is enacted, all the stakeholders are caught up in the virtuous circle we described at the beginning of this book. If you and your colleagues in your district, working with other like-minded colleagues in a few other districts and a handful of universities, can begin this transformation, there is every reason to believe that others will join you and others will follow them. Why? Because it works. We know it works because millions of schoolchildren around the world who have been educated in systems using this model are performing at very high levels. So can yours. And when they do, others will notice.

Bibliography

Alberta Education. (2010). *Inspiring education: A dialogue with Albertans.* Edmonton, Alberta, Canada: Government of Alberta, Ministry of Education.

Allegretto, S., & Mishel, L. (2016). *The teacher pay gap is wider: Teachers' pay continues to fall further behind pay of comparable workers.* Washington, DC: Economic Policy Institute.

Barber, M., & Mourshad, M. (2007). *How the world's best performing systems come out on top.* San Francisco: McKinsey & Company.

Brynjolfsson, E., & McAffee, A. (2014). *The second machine age: Work, progress, and prosperity in a time of brilliant technologies.* New York and London: W. W. Norton.

Bull, R., & Bautista, A. (forthcoming). *International case studies of innovative early childhood systems: The early advantage in Singapore.* Retrieved from http://ncee.org/what-we-do/center-on-international-education-benchmarking/cieb-supported-research/

Burns, D., & McIntyre, A. (2017). *Empowered educators in Australia: How high-performing systems shape teaching quality.* San Francisco: Jossey-Bass/Wiley.

Commission on the Skills of the American Workforce. (1990). *America's choice: High skills or low wages!* Rochester, NY: National Center on Education and the Economy.

Darling-Hammond, L., Burns, D., Campbell, C., Goodwin, A. L., Hammerness, K., Ling Low, E. E., McIntyre, A., Sato, M., & Zeichner, K. (2017). *Empowered educators: How high-performing systems shape teaching quality around the world.* San Francisco: Jossey-Bass/Wiley.

Darling-Hammond, L., Goodwin, L., & Low, E. (2017). *Empowered educators in Singapore: How high-performing systems shape teaching quality.* San Francisco: Jossey-Bass/Wiley.

Desmond, M. (2016). *Evicted: Poverty and profit in the American city*. New York: Crown Publishing.

Drucker, P. F. (1969). *The age of discontinuity*. New York: HarperCollins.

The Economist. (2016). Automation and anxiety: Will smarter machines cause mass unemployment? Retrieved from https://www.economist.com/news/special-report/21700758-will-smarter-machines-cause-mass-unemployment-automation-and-anxiety

Egalite, A., Kisida, B., & Winters, M. (2015). Representation in the classroom: The effect of own-race teachers on student achievement. *Economics of Education Review, 45*, 44–52.

Eiter, M. (2002). Best practices in leadership development: Lessons from the best business schools and corporate universities. In M. Tucker & J. Codding (Eds.), *The principal challenge: Leading and managing schools in an era of accountability* (pp. 99–122). San Francisco: Jossey-Bass/Wiley.

Ford, M. (2015). *The rise of the robots: Technology and the threat of a jobless future*. New York: Basic Books.

Friedman, T. (2007). *The world is flat: A brief history of the twenty-first century*. New York: Farrar, Strauss, and Giroux.

Fullan, M., & Quinn, J. (2015). *Coherence: The right drivers for action in schools, districts and systems*. Toronto: Corwin and Ontario Principals Council.

Gang, D. (Ed.). (2010). *National survey and policy analysis for teacher professional development in primary and secondary schools*. Shanghai: East China Normal University Press.

Gladwell, M. (2008). *Outliers: The story of success*. New York: Little, Brown and Co.

Goldhaber, D., & Walsh, J. (2014). *Rhetoric versus reality: Is the academic caliber of the teacher workforce changing?* Seattle, WA: Center for Education Data and Research.

Goldin, C., & Katz, L. (2008). *The race between education and technology*. Cambridge, MA: Harvard University Press.

Goodman, M., Sands, A., & Coley, R. (2017). *America's skills challenge: Millennials and the future*. Princeton, NJ: Educational Testing Service.

Goodwin, L. (2017). *Empowered educators in Singapore: How high-performing systems shape teaching quality*. San Francisco: Jossey-Bass/Wiley.

Hammerness, K., Ahtiainen, R., & Sahlberg, P. (2017). *Empowered educators in Finland: How high-performing systems shape teaching quality*. San Francisco: Jossey-Bass/Wiley.

Harari, Y. N. (2017). *Homo deus: A brief history of tomorrow*. New York: HarperCollins.

Haynes, M. (2014). *On the path to equity: Improving the effectiveness of beginning teachers*. Washington, DC: Alliance for Excellent Education.

Holley, P. (2015, January 29). Bill Gates on dangers of artificial intelligence: "I don't understand why some people are not concerned." *Washington Post*.

Retrieved from https://www.washingtonpost.com/news/the-switch/wp/ 2015/01/28/bill-gates-on-dangers-of-artificial-intelligence-dont-understand- why-some-people-are-not-concerned/?utm_term=.19ffaea72ed4

Ingersoll, R. (2003). *Is there really a teacher shortage?* Philadelphia: University of Pennsylvania, Consortium for Policy Research in Education.

Ingersoll, R., & Perda, D. (2014). *How high is teacher turnover and is it a problem?* Philadelphia: University of Pennsylvania, Consortium for Policy Research in Education.

Jensen, B., Downing, P., & Clark, A. (2017). *Preparing to lead: Lessons in princi- pal development from high-performing education systems.* Washington, DC: National Center on Education and the Economy.

Kahlenberg, R. D. (2007). *Tough liberal: Albert Shanker and the battles over schools, unions, race, and democracy.* New York: Columbia University Press.

Kirp, D.L. (2013). *Improbable scholars: The rebirth of a great American school system and a strategy for America's schools.* New York: Oxford University Press.

Krugman, P. (2014, November 12). On income stagnation. *The New York Times.* Retrieved from https://krugman.blogs.nytimes.com/2014/11/12/on-income- stagnation/

Kumpailanen, K. (forthcoming). *International case studies of innovative early childhood systems: The early advantage in Finland.* Retrieved from http:// ncee.org/what-we-do/center-on-international-education-benchmarking/ cieb-supported-research/

Kurzweil, R. (2005). *The singularity is near.* New York: Penguin Books.

Learning Policy Institute. (2017). *What's the cost of teacher turnover?* Retrieved from https://learningpolicyinstitute.org/product/the-cost-of-teacher-turnover

Levy, F., & Murnane, R. (2004). *The new division of labor: How computers are creating the next job market.* Princeton, NJ: Princeton University Press.

Long, C. (2016, January 20). How high-performing nations treat educators as professionals. *NEA Today.* Retrieved from http://neatoday.org/2016/01/20/ high-performing-nations-professional-development/

Manyika, J., Chui, M., Miremadi, M., Bughin, J., George, K., Willmott, P., & Dewhurst, M. (2017). *Harnessing automation for a future that works.* San Francisco: McKinsey Global Institute, McKinsey & Company.

McCorduck, P. (2004). *Machines who think: A personal inquiry into the history and prospects of artificial intelligence.* Natick, MA: AK Peters Ltd.

McGregor, D. (1960). *The Human Side of Enterprise.* New York: McGraw-Hill.

McGregor, D. (1967). *The Professional Manager.* New York: McGraw-Hill.

Mullis, I. V. S., Martin, M. O., Foy, P., & Hooper, M. (2016). *TIMSS 2015 international results in mathematics.* Boston: Boston College, Lynch School of Education, TIMSS & PIRLS International Study Center.

Murray, C. (2012). *Coming apart.* New York: Crown Forum.

National Center on Education and the Economy. (2013). *What does it really mean to be college and work ready?* Washington, DC: Author.

National Center on Education and the Economy. (2018). *How does Maryland stack up? A gap analysis comparing Maryland to international and domestic top performers.* Produced for the Maryland Commission on Innovation and Excellence in Education.

National Conference of State Legislatures. (2016). *No time to lose.* Denver, CO: Author.

National Institute of Education. (2009). *A teacher education model for the 21st century: A report by the National Institute of Education.* Singapore: Author.

Nunnery, J. A., Ross, S. M., Chappell, S., Pribesh, S., & Hoag-Carhart, E. (2011). *The impact of the NISL executive development program on performance in Massachusetts: Cohort 2 results.* Norfolk, VA: Old Dominion University, Center for Educational Partnerships.

Nunnery, J. A., Yen, C., & Ross, S. (2011). *Effects of the National Institute for School Leadership's executive development program on school performance in Pennsylvania: 2006–2010 pilot cohort results.* Norfolk, VA: Old Dominion University, Center for Educational Partnerships.

OECD. (2000). *Knowledge and skills for life: Results from the OECD PISA 2000.* Paris: OECD Publishing.

OECD. (2010). *Strong performers and successful reformers.* Paris: OECD Publishing.

OECD. (2014a). *PISA 2012 results in focus: What 15-year-olds know and what they can do with what they know.* Paris: OECD Publishing.

OECD. (2014b). *TALIS 2013 results: An international perspective on teaching and learning.* Paris: OECD Publishing.

OECD. (2015). *Helping immigrant students to succeed at school—and beyond.* Paris: OECD Publishing.

OECD. (2016a). *Education at a glance 2016: OECD indicators.* Paris: OECD Publishing.

OECD. (2016b). *PISA 2015 results (volume I): Excellence and equity in education, PISA.* Paris: OECD Publishing.

OECD. (2017a). *Education at a glance 2017: OECD indicators.* Paris: OECD Publishing.

OECD. (2017b). PISA 2018 participants. Retrieved from http://www.oecd.org/pisa/aboutpisa/pisa-2018-participants.htm

OECDStat. (2017). Income distribution and poverty, by country. Retrieved from http://stats.oecd.org/index.aspx?queryid=66670

Putnam, R. (2015). *Our kids: The American dream in crisis.* New York: Simon & Schuster.

Rivkin, S. G., Hanushek, E., & Kain, J. F. (2005). Teachers, schools, and academic achievement. *Econometrica, 73*(2), 417–458.

Sang-Hun, C., & Markoff, J. (2016, March 9). Master of Go board game is walloped by Google computer program. *The New York Times*.

Sato, M. (2017). *Empowered educators in China: How high-performing systems shape teaching quality*. San Francisco: Jossey-Bass/Wiley.

Sharkey, P., & Graham, B. (2013). *Mobility and the metropolis: How communities factor into economic mobility*. Philadelphia: Pew Charitable Trusts.

Singapore Academy of Corporate Management. (2014). Education in Singapore. Retrieved from http://www.singapore-academy.org/index.php/en/education/library-media-center/singapore-presentation/item/217-education-in-singapore

Statistics Canada. (2011). Immigration and ethnocultural diversity in Canada. Retrieved from http://www12.statcan.gc.ca/nhs-enm/2011/as-sa/99-010-x/99-010-x2011001-eng.cfm#a2

Stewart, V. 2010. *How Singapore developed a high quality teacher workforce*. New York: The Asia Society.

Stiglitz, J. (2012). *The price of inequality: How today's divided society endangers our future*. New York: W. W. Norton.

Swanson, B., & Mandel, M. (2017, May 14). Robots will save the economy. *The Wall Street Journal*.

Temin, P. (2017). *The vanishing class: Prejudice and power in a dual economy*. Cambridge, MA: MIT Press.

TNTP. 2015. *The mirage: Confronting the hard truth about our quest for teacher development*. Washington, DC: Author.

Tucker, M. (2011). *Surpassing Shanghai: An agenda for American education built on the world's leading systems*. Cambridge, MA: Harvard Education Press.

Tucker, M. (2012). *The phoenix: Vocational education and training in Singapore*. Washington, DC: National Center on Education and the Economy.

Tucker, M. (2016a). *9 Building blocks for a world-class education system*. Washington, DC: National Center on Education and the Economy. Retrieved from http://ncee.org/9buildingblocks/

Tucker, M. (2016b, June 23). High poverty and high achievement in Hong Kong. *Education Week*. Retrieved from http://blogs.edweek.org/edweek/top_performers/2016/06/high_poverty_high_achievement_in_hong_kong.html

Tucker, M. (2017). Education for a digital future: The challenge. *Future frontiers: Education for an AI world*. New South Wales, Australia: Melbourne University Press and the New South Wales Department of Education. Retrieved from https://education.nsw.gov.au/our-priorities/innovate-for-the-future/education-for-a-changing-world/media/documents/future-frontiers-education-for-an-ai-world/Future_Frontiers-Text.pdf

Tucker, M., & Codding, J. (2002). *The principal challenge: Leading and managing schools in an era of accountability*. San Francisco: Jossey-Bass.

Tyack, D., & Cuban, L. (1995). *Tinkering toward utopia: A century of public school reform*. Cambridge, MA: Harvard University Press.

U.S. Department of Education. (2012). *The nation's report card: NAEP 2012 long-term trends in academic progress.* Washington, DC: U.S. Department of Education, Institute of Education Sciences, National Center for Education Statistics.

U.S. Department of Education. (2013). *The nation's report card: A first look: 2013 mathematics and reading.* Washington, DC: U.S. Department of Education, Institute of Education Sciences, National Center for Education Statistics.

U.S. Department of Education. (2014). *Equitable access to quality educators: State equity profiles.* Washington, DC: Author.

U.S. Department of Education. (2015a). *The nation's report card: 2015 mathematics and reading assessments.* Washington, DC: U.S. Department of Education, Institute of Education Sciences, National Center for Education Statistics. Retrieved from https://www.nationsreportcard.gov/reading_math_2015/#?grade=4

U.S. Department of Education, National Center for Education Statistics. (2015b). *Public school teacher attrition and mobility in the first five years: Results from the first through fifth waves of the 2007–08 beginning teacher longitudinal study.* Washington, DC: Author.

U.S. Department of Education, National Center for Education Statistics. (2017a). *Adult training and education: Results from the National Household Education Surveys Program of 2016.* Washington, DC: U.S. Department of Education.

U.S. Department of Education, National Center for Education Statistics. (2017b). *Digest of education statistics.* Washington, DC: U.S. Department of Education.

U.S. Department of Labor, Bureau of Labor Statistics. (n.d.). *Labor force participation rate 1970–2015: Ages 16 and over, seasonally adjusted.* Retrieved from https://data.bls.gov/pdq/SurveyOutputServlet

Vance, A. (2015). *Elon musk: Tesla, Space X, and the quest for a fantastic future.* New York: Ecco-HarperCollins.

Wilson, W. J. (1987). *The truly disadvantaged: The inner city, the underclass, and public policy.* Chicago: University of Chicago Press.

Xiaoyan, L., Kidwai, H., & Zhang, M. (2016). *How Shanghai does it: Insights and lessons from the highest-ranking education system in the world.* Washington, DC: World Bank

Yoon, K. S., Duncan, T., Lee, S. W.-Y., Scarloss, B., & Shapley, K. (2007). *Reviewing the evidence on how teacher professional development affects student achievement* (Issues & Answers Report, REL 2007–No. 033). Washington, DC: U.S. Department of Education, Institute of Education Sciences, National Center for Education Evaluation and Regional Assistance, Regional Educational Laboratory Southwest.

Zhang, M., Ding, X., & Xu, J. (2016). *Developing Shanghai's teachers.* Washington, DC: National Center on Education and the Economy.

Index

Note: The letter *f* following a page number denotes a figure.

About the Author

Marc Tucker is the founder, CEO, and president of the National Center on Education and the Economy. A leader of the standards-driven education reform movement, Tucker has been studying the strategies used by the countries with the most successful education systems for three decades. He created New Standards—a precursor to the Common Core, the National Board for Professional Teaching Standards, the Commission on the Skills of the American Workforce, and its successor, the New Commission on the Skills of the American Workforce; and he was instrumental in creating the National Skill Standards Board. Tucker also created the National Institute of School Leadership.

Tucker authored the 1986 Carnegie report *A Nation Prepared: Teachers for the 21st Century* and the report of the Commission on the Skills of the American Workforce, *America's Choice: High Skills or Low Wages,* and was the lead author of *Tough Choices or Tough Times,* the report of the New Commission on the Skills of the American Workforce. He coauthored or edited *Thinking for a Living: Education and the Wealth of Nations; Standards for Our Schools: How to Set Them, Measure Them, and Reach Them;* and *The Principal Challenge.*

Tucker was commended by President Bill Clinton for his contributions to the design of the Clinton administration's education and job-training proposals in the Rose Garden ceremony celebrating the passage of the legislation authorizing the Clinton program. In 2014, he received the James Bryant Conant Award from the Education Commission of the States for his outstanding individual contribution to American education.

About the Sponsoring Organizations

CENTER ON INTERNATIONAL
EDUCATION BENCHMARKING
LEARNING FROM THE WORLD'S HIGH PERFORMING EDUCATION SYSTEMS

The Center on International Education Benchmarking®, a program of NCEE, funds and conducts research around the world on the most successful education systems to identify the strategies those countries have used to produce their superior performance. Through its books, reports, website, monthly newsletter, and a weekly update of education news around the world, CIEB provides up-to-date information and analysis on those countries whose students regularly top the PISA league tables. Visit www.ncee.org/cieb to learn more.

The National Center on Education and the Economy was created in 1988 to analyze the implications of changes in the international economy for American education, formulate an agenda for American education based on that analysis, and seek wherever possible to accomplish that agenda through policy change and development of the resources educators would need to carry it out. For more information visit www.ncee.org.

Related ASCD Resources

At the time of publication, the following resources were available (ASCD stock numbers appear in parentheses):

Print Products

Curriculum 21: Essential Education for a Changing World edited by Heidi Hayes Jacobs (#109008)

A World-Class Education: Learning from International Models of Excellence and Innovation by Vivien Stewart (#111016)

Catching Up or Leading the Way: American Education in the Age of Globalization by Yong Zhao (#109076)

Transforming Schools: Creating a Culture of Continuous Improvement by Allison Zmuda, Robert Kuklis and Everett Kline (#103112)

Promises Kept: Sustaining School and District Leadership in a Turbulent Era by Steven Jay Gross (#101078)

Schooling by Design: Mission, Action, and Achievement by Grant Wiggins and Jay McTighe (#107018)

Teachers Wanted: Attracting and Retaining Good Teachers by Daniel A. Heller (#104005)

Leading with Focus: Elevating the Essentials for School and District Improvement by Mike Schmoker (#116024)

Sustaining Change in Schools: How to Overcome Differences and Focus on Quality by Daniel P. Johnson (#105006)

Balanced Leadership for Powerful Learning: Tools for Achieving Success in Your School by Bryan Goodwin and Greg Cameron with Heather Hein (#112025)

Align the Design: A Blueprint for School Improvement by Nancy J. Mooney and Ann T. Mausbach (#108005)

West Meets East: Best Practices from Expert Teachers in the U.S. and China by Leslie Grant, James Stronge, Xianxuan Xu, Patricia Popp, Yaling Sun, and Catherine Little (#111012)

Five Levers to Improve Learning: How to Prioritize for Powerful Results in Your School by Tony Frontier and Jim Rickabaugh (#114002)

What Makes a World-Class School and How We Can Get There by James H. Stronge with Xianxuan Xu (#117078)

Leading Change Together: Developing Educator Capacity Within Schools and Systems by Eleanor E. Drago-Severson and Jessica Blum-DeStefano (#117027)

For up-to-date information about ASCD resources, go to www.ascd.org. You can search the complete archives of *Educational Leadership* at www.ascd.org/el.

ASCD myTeachSource®

Download resources from a professional learning platform with hundreds of research-based best practices and tools for your classroom at http://myteachsource.ascd.org/.

For more information, send an e-mail to member@ascd.org; call 1-800-933-2723 or 703-578-9600; send a fax to 703-575-5400; or write to Information Services, ASCD, 1703 N. Beauregard St., Alexandria, VA 22311-1714 USA.